SALT GRILL

FINE DINING FOR THE WHOLE FAMILY

SALT GRILL

FINE DINING FOR THE WHOLE FAMILY
LUKE MANGAN

MURDOCH BOOKS

CONTENTS

INTRODUCTION

Anyone who has ever eaten in one of my restaurants — going back to the first Salt which opened in Darlinghurst in 1999 — will know I'm not one for hiding in the kitchen.

Sure, I love to cook, and I love to create menus, but having done the cooking, I want to get out and see that you, my customers, are enjoying the food me and my kitchen team have prepared. It's one of the ways I can share in your experience. And sharing is what this book is about.

Many of the recipes are designed to be shared in a couple of ways, ways that we in Australia have incorporated into our own food culture.

One is the Chinese way: the big plate in the middle of the table to be shared by everybody at the table. In the mains section, you'll find share dishes like Pan-fried Potato Gnocchi with Summer Vegetables and Baked Flathead with Prosciutto, Tomato and Parsley.

The other is with small plates, the tapas idea, borrowed from Spain. You may like to serve tapas instead of a first course, with an aperitif before the main meal, either at the table, or in the garden. Or replace the three course main meal with a lot of little dishes. The tapas phenomenon is more than just another food fad: it's another stage in the evolution of our eating habits.

That's the inspiration for dishes like Roasted Capsicum & White Anchovies on Toast, and Oyster Tempura with Leek and Wasabi. The idea is Spanish but the food comes from all over. Our tapas were so popular they inspired the first Salt tapas & bar in Singapore with a second to open soon in the Sentosa boutique hotel at Seminyak in Bali.

I'm also sharing some recipes that offer simple twists on old favourites like Orange Lamingtons, Rum Raisin and Chocolate Bread and Butter pudding and a Waldorf Salad with Bresaola: and untwisted standards like Lobster Thermidor, Salt and Pepper Squid and Floating Islands.

And you'll find the signature dishes that are the foundation of our menus: Sashimi of Kingfish, Liquorice Parfait and glass brasserie's Sydney Crab Omelette, among others.

Another aspect of sharing is making sure that these recipes are, on the whole, home cook and kitchen friendly. You won't find anything molecular in here: this is a foam-free book. Open the book on any page, and if you love to cook, you'll be able to cook the recipes you find there.

When I opened the first Salt in Darlinghurst, I did have some clever dishes on the menu. That was then — I was trying to prove myself. But that's okay, it gave me a benchmark. Now, I don't want to do an eight course degustation. Today, I cook food I can eat right now. Food based on freshness and the best ingredients you can find. That hasn't changed. Today, all the Salt grills — on P&O cruise ships, in Singapore, Jakarta and Surfer's Paradise — stick to that simple philosophy.

As do all the recipes in this book. I hope they inspire you to cook for those you care for, and add pleasure to your table.

I love the whole concept of sharing food. It's a perfect way to interact with friends and allows you to try a variety of dishes at your favourite restaurant or bar, rather than just being limited to a starter and a main.

Often when I dine at restaurants I will order a few starters one at a time and share them at the table.

The tapas recipes in this chapter are really quite simple, and will help you turn your kitchen into a little tapas bar so you can enjoy a similar experience at home!

Rounding out this chapter is a terrific selection of bread recipes. I think my love for bread came about when I was fourteen. Our family had a little beach house in a small seaside town that happened to have an incredible local bakery. Dad would always take me down on a Sunday morning around 7 am and we would stand in the queue for a loaf of crusty white bread that was still warm from the old wood-fired ovens — just amazing.

I'd strongly recommend investing in a good pair of kitchen scales — they will stand you in good stead when baking the breads in this chapter. For the best results, weigh every ingredient when baking and your bread (and guests!) will reap the benefits.

I have always loved the smell and taste of freshly baked bread. You can't beat it!

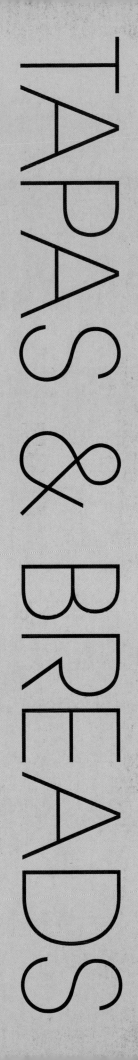

TAPAS & BREADS

ROASTED CAPSICUM &
WHITE ANCHOVIES ON TOAST

makes 8 pieces

ingredients

3 yellow capsicums (peppers)
3 red capsicums (peppers)
80 ml (2½ fl oz/⅓ cup) extra virgin
    olive oil, plus extra for drizzling
100 g (3½ oz) French shallots, diced
6 garlic cloves, thinly sliced
55 g (2 oz/¼ cup) caster
    (superfine) sugar
50 ml (1¾ fl oz) cabernet sauvignon
    vinegar or red wine vinegar
150 g (5½ oz) sultanas (golden raisins)
8 baguette slices
16 white anchovies (see note)
2 tablespoons flat-leaf (Italian)
    parsley leaves

method

Preheat the oven to 200°C (400°F/Gas 6).

Place the capsicums in a roasting tin, drizzle with some extra virgin olive oil and season with sea salt and freshly ground black pepper. Bake for 15–20 minutes, or until the skins have blistered.

Place the capsicums in a bowl, cover with plastic wrap and allow to sweat in their skins for 30 minutes. Remove the plastic wrap. Remove the seeds and membranes from the capsicums, then scrape off the skin. Slice the flesh into thin strips and set aside.

Place a saucepan over medium heat. Add the shallot, garlic and the 80 ml (2½ fl oz/⅓ cup) olive oil and cook, without colouring, for 3–5 minutes, or until the shallot and garlic have become translucent.

Sprinkle with the sugar and stir to make a light caramel, then stir in the vinegar to deglaze the pan. Add the capsicum strips and cook for about 3 minutes, then add the sultanas and cook for a further 3 minutes.

Remove from the heat, season to taste, then place in a bowl to keep warm.

Drizzle the baguette slices with extra virgin olive oil. Chargrill or toast the slices, then arrange on a serving tray.

Divide the capsicum mixture among the toasts, arrange the anchovies on top and garnish with the parsley.

Drizzle with a little more olive oil and serve.

note: Popular in Spain and other Mediterranean regions, white anchovies (also called boquerones or gavros) are gently marinated in a vinegar mixture rather than cured in salty brine, and have a more mellow flavour and a much paler colour than regular anchovies. You'll find them packed in tins or jars at good delicatessens and fine food stores.

MARINATED OLIVES & FETA

serves 20–25

marinated feta
300 ml (10½ fl oz) good-quality
    extra virgin olive oil
8 fresh bay leaves
15 thyme sprigs
1 tablespoon black peppercorns
5 rosemary sprigs
500 g (1 lb 2 oz) soft feta cheese,
    cubed

marinated olives
1 kg (2 lb 4 oz) good-quality
    unpitted black olives
1 kg (2 lb 4 oz) good-quality
    unpitted green olives
25 lime leaves
5 chillies, mild to hot
2 tablespoons coriander seeds
100 g (3½ oz) flat-leaf (Italian)
    parsley, with stalks
2 tablespoons black peppercorns
8 fresh bay leaves
8–10 thyme sprigs
1½ cups roughly chopped coriander
    (cilantro) leaves and stems
4 lemons, peeled
6 lime peel strips
10 garlic cloves, peeled and cut
    in half lengthways
1 litre (35 fl oz/4 cups) good-quality
    extra virgin olive oil

for the marinated feta
Place the olive oil, bay leaves, thyme, peppercorns and rosemary in a saucepan and bring up to a medium heat.
    Remove from the heat and leave to cool to room temperature.
    Place the feta in a clean container and pour the oil mixture over. Cover and marinate in the refrigerator for 24–48 hours.
    Remove the feta from the fridge 1–2 hours before serving. Serve at room temperature.

for the marinated olives
Wash the brine off the olives, then strain and set aside.
    Place all the remaining ingredients in a saucepan and bring up to a medium heat — do not boil.
    Add the olives and again bring back to a medium heat.
    Remove from the heat, cover with plastic wrap and set aside until cold.
    Place the olive mixture in a clean container and marinate in the fridge for 24 hours. Keep refrigerated until ready to use.
    Remove the olives from the fridge 1–2 hours before serving. Serve at room temperature.

for the chipotle mayonnaise

Blend the chipotle chilli in a food processor with the olive oil, then pass it through a sieve into a small bowl. Mix the mayonnaise and lime juice through, then cover with plastic wrap and keep in the fridge.

for the prawn mix

Place the prawn meat in a food processor and blend to a smooth paste.

Add the remaining prawn mix ingredients and briefly blend until just combined. Transfer to a clean container, then cover and refrigerate.

for the corn salsa

Place the corn cobs in a saucepan of simmering water and cook for 5 minutes. Remove the corn and place in iced water until cool enough to handle.

Remove the corn from the water. Cut the kernels off the cobs and place in a bowl.

Add the remaining corn salsa ingredients and mix well. Season with sea salt and freshly ground black pepper.

for the toasts

Fill a deep-fryer or large heavy-based saucepan one-third full of vegetable oil and heat the oil to 180°C (350°F), or until a cube of bread dropped into the oil turns golden brown in 15 seconds.

Meanwhile, spread the prawn mix evenly over the top of the bread slices. Coat in the sesame seeds, then cut each slice into two pieces down the middle.

Place half the toasts in the deep-fryer and cook for 1 minute. Turn them over with tongs and cook for another minute. Drain briefly on paper towels and season to taste.

Repeat with the remaining toasts.

Serve the toasts warm, topped with the corn salsa and chipotle mayonnaise.

note: A signature spice in Mexican and Tex-Mex cuisine, smoked chipotle chillies are simply smoke-dried jalapeño peppers. They are available both whole as whole dried chillies and as a ground powder, from spice shops and good delicatessens.

ingredients

10 slices white bread, crusts cut off
100 g (3½ oz/⅔ cup) sesame seeds
vegetable oil, for deep-frying

chipotle mayonnaise

2 teaspoons tinned smoked chipotle chilli (see note)
2 tablespoons extra virgin olive oil
100 g (3½ oz) mayonnaise
juice of ½ lime

prawn mix

400 g (14 oz) prawn (shrimp) meat
1 tablespoon chopped fresh ginger
2 garlic cloves, chopped
1 teaspoon sugar
1 free-range egg white
2 teaspoons sesame oil
30 g (1 oz/¼ cup) finely chopped spring onion (scallion)
1 tablespoon fish sauce
1 teaspoon sea salt

corn salsa

2 corn cobs
50 g (1¾ oz/½ cup) diced French shallots
½ teaspoon smoked paprika
30 g (1 oz/1 cup) coriander (cilantro) leaves, chopped
juice of ½ lime
60 ml (2 fl oz/¼ cup) extra virgin olive oil

ARANCINI WITH TALEGGIO & GREEN GODDESS DRESSING

makes 30

for the mushroom duxelle

Heat a large frying pan over medium–high heat. Add the olive oil and mushrooms and sauté for 5–7 minutes, or until there is no juice left. Add the thyme and wine and cook until there is no liquid remaining.

Remove from the heat and discard the thyme sprigs.

Blend finely in a food processor and season to taste.

for the mushroom risotto

Heat a heavy-based saucepan over medium–low heat. Add the olive oil and half the butter. Add the onion, leek and garlic and sauté without browning for 8–10 minutes.

Add the rice and sauté until the rice is translucent, taking care not to brown the mixture. Stir in the wine and cook until it has evaporated. Slowly add the hot stock and cook for 20–25 minutes, or until the rice is cooked all the way through, stirring at intervals — do not allow to boil.

Remove from the heat and stir in the mushroom duxelle, parmesan, chopped herbs, remaining butter and the truffle oil. Season to taste. Spread the mixture on a tray, then cover with plastic wrap and cool in the refrigerator for 1 hour.

Remove from the fridge and mix the taleggio through, then shape into 30 balls of equal size. Using damp hands, roll the risotto balls in the flour, then the egg and milk mixture, and finally the breadcrumbs.

Fill a deep-fryer or large heavy-based saucepan one-third full of vegetable oil and heat the oil to 180°C (350°F), or until a cube of bread dropped into the oil turns golden brown in 15 seconds.

Add the risotto balls in three to four batches. Cook each batch for 3–5 minutes, or until golden, draining each batch on paper towels.

to serve

Drizzle the green goddess dressing on each serving plate and top with the warm arancini. Sprinkle with a little parmesan, drizzle with some truffle oil and serve.

note: Taleggio is a soft Italian washed-rind cheese with lovely melting qualities, a fruity tang and a pungent aroma. You'll find it in shops where specialty cheeses are sold.

ingredients

1 quantity Green Goddess Dressing
(see recipe on page 200)
parmesan cheese, for sprinkling
truffle oil, for drizzling

mushroom duxelle

50 ml (1¾ fl oz) extra virgin olive oil
250 g (9 oz) Swiss brown mushrooms,
sliced
4–5 thyme sprigs
1 litre (35 fl oz/4 cups) red wine

mushroom risotto

150 ml (5 fl oz) extra virgin olive oil
150 g (5½ oz) cold unsalted butter
½ small onion, finely diced
100 g (3½ oz) leeks, white part only, diced
3 garlic cloves, chopped
250 g (9 oz) carnaroli or arborio rice
200 ml (7 fl oz) red wine
2 litres (70 fl oz/8 cups) hot
vegetable stock
250 g (9 oz) Mushroom Duxelle
(see above)
50 g (1¾ oz/½ cup) finely grated
parmesan cheese
4 tablespoons chopped tarragon
4–6 tablespoons chopped chervil
200 ml (7 fl oz) truffle oil
200 g (7 oz) taleggio cheese
(see note), diced
50 g (1¾ oz/⅓ cup) plain
(all-purpose) flour
3 free-range eggs, whisked with
a splash of milk
150 g (5½ oz) dry or fresh breadcrumbs
vegetable oil, for deep-frying

SALT & PEPPER SQUID

serves 6

ingredients
vegetable oil, for deep-frying
600 g (1 lb 5 oz) squid tubes and
    tentacles, cleaned
baby watercress sprigs, to garnish
lemon wedges, to serve

spice mix
110 g (3¾ oz/¾ cup) plain
    (all-purpose) flour
3 teaspoons sea salt
2 teaspoons ground white pepper
2 teaspoons Chinese five-spice
1 teaspoon chilli powder

lemon and caper mayonnaise
300 g (10½ oz/1¼ cups) mayonnaise
1 tablespoon chopped capers
50 ml (1¾ fl oz) lemon juice

for the spice mix
Combine the spice mix ingredients in a bowl. Mix well and set aside.

for the lemon and caper mayonnaise
Mix together the mayonnaise, capers and lemon juice. Season with sea salt and ground white pepper, then spoon into a serving bowl, suitable for a platter. Set aside.

Fill a deep-fryer or large heavy-based saucepan one-third full of vegetable oil and heat the oil to 190°C (375°F), or until a cube of bread dropped into the oil turns golden brown in 10 seconds.

Meanwhile, using a sharp knife, cut through one side of each squid tube, lengthways. Open the squid out flat, with the inside surface facing up, then score the surface diagonally, to make a crisscross pattern. Cut the squid into 3.5 cm (1½ inch) squares and pat dry with paper towels.

Add the squid squares and tentacles to the spice mix and toss gently to coat. Remove half the squid from the spice mix and shake off any excess.

Add the squid to the hot oil and cook, turning with a slotted metal spoon, for 2 minutes, or until the squid is golden in colour and curls.

Using the slotted spoon, transfer the squid to a large plate lined with paper towels and leave to drain. Reheat the oil, then cook the remaining squid in the same way.

to serve
Transfer the warm squid to a serving platter. Garnish with baby watercress and serve immediately, with lemon wedges and the lemon and caper mayonnaise.

TROUT RILLETTE WITH SPICED BEETROOT

serves 4–6

for the spiced beetroot

Add the olive oil and spices to a saucepan and toast over medium–low heat for 1 minute, or until fragrant, taking care that the spices don't burn.

Add the beetroot and sauté for 5–6 minutes, or until tender. Drizzle with a little vinegar, season with sea salt and freshly ground black pepper, then remove from the heat and leave to cool. Cover and set aside until needed.

for the trout rillette

Place the raw trout on a tray and rub in the Pernod and some sea salt. Cover and marinate for 2 hours.

Steam the smoked trout in a steamer for 2–3 minutes, then remove from the steamer and leave to cool.

Place the shallot and olive oil in a saucepan and cook, without browning, over medium–low heat for 5 minutes. Remove to a bowl and leave to cool.

Add the remaining rillette ingredients to the sautéed shallot. Mix together well, then season to taste.

to serve

Divide the trout rillette among serving jars or dishes and place the spiced beetroot on top. Garnish with baby celery cress leaves and serve with warm brioche.

note: Chaat masala is a tangy spice mix widely used throughout India and Pakistan. Particular blends vary, but dried mango (amchoor powder) is a signature ingredient. You'll find chaat masala in spice shops and South Asian grocery stores.

ingredients

baby celery cress or celery leaves, to garnish
warm Brioche (see recipe on page 31), to serve

spiced beetroot

1 tablespoon extra virgin olive oil
½ teaspoon chaat masala (see note)
½ teaspoon ground cumin
½ teaspoon ground coriander
125 g (4½ oz) red beetroot (beets), peeled, washed and finely grated
splash of cabernet sauvignon vinegar or red wine vinegar

trout rillette

300 g (10½ oz) skinless, boneless raw trout
1 tablespoon Pernod
200 g (7 oz) skinless, boneless smoked trout, diced
70 g (2½ oz/⅔ cup) very finely diced French shallots
1 tablespoon extra virgin olive oil
125 g (4½ oz) butter, whipped using electric beaters
1 tablespoon crème fraîche
1½ tablespoons lemon juice

OYSTER TEMPURA WITH LEEK & WASABI

makes 12

ingredients

625 g (1 lb 6 oz/2 cups) rock salt,
    for serving the oysters on
12 freshly shucked oysters, on the
    half-shell
80 g (2¾ oz/¾ cup) julienned leek,
    white part only
vegetable oil, for deep-frying
rice flour, for dusting the oysters
50 ml (1¾ fl oz) Soy and Wasabi
    Dressing (see below)
1 sheet nori (dried seaweed),
    roughly torn

soy and wasabi dressing

2 tablespoons wasabi paste
50 ml (1¾ fl oz) hot water
3 teaspoons sesame oil
250 ml (9 fl oz/1 cup) olive oil
2 tablespoons soy sauce

tempura batter

75 g (2½ oz/½ cup) rice flour
75 g (2½ oz/½ cup) tapioca flour
125–150 ml (4–5 fl oz) soda water
juice of ½ lemon
juice of ½ lime
1–2 ice cubes

Near serving time, spread the rock salt on a serving platter. Remove the oysters from their shells and set aside on a tray.

Wash the oyster shells, pat dry, then arrange on top of the rock salt platter.

Add the leek to a saucepan of simmering water and blanch for about 30 seconds. Remove and refresh in iced water. Drain the leek on paper towels, then place in a bowl.

for the soy and wasabi dressing

Place the wasabi paste in a bowl with half the hot water. Gradually add the sesame oil and olive oil and slowly whisk, adding the soy sauce and remaining hot water until the mixture has emulsified. Cover and set aside.

for the tempura batter

Place the rice flour and tapioca flour in a bowl. Slowly add the soda water, lemon juice and lime juice and lightly mix with a fork until you have a thick batter.

Add the ice to the batter. The ice will melt and thin your batter until you have the right consistency — the batter should just coat your finger.

Fill a deep-fryer or large heavy-based saucepan one-third full of vegetable oil and heat the oil to 170°C (325°F), or until a cube of bread dropped into the oil turns golden brown in 20 seconds.

Dust the oysters in the rice flour and pat off any excess. Coat the oysters in the tempura batter, then gently drop them into the deep-fryer.

Cook for no longer than 30–40 seconds, as oysters can overcook very quickly. Remove from the oil and briefly drain on paper towels.

to serve

Mix the leek with half the soy and wasabi dressing and place in the oyster shells. Drizzle with the remaining dressing. Place the tempura oysters in the shells and garnish with the nori. Serve immediately, while still warm.

CHARGRILLED MACKEREL, PICKLED ONION & FENNEL ON TOAST

serves 6

for the pickled onions

Place all the ingredients, except the onion, in a saucepan and bring to the boil. Remove from the heat and allow to stand for 1 hour.

After 1 hour, place the saucepan back on the heat and bring back to the boil. Place the onion in a metal bowl, then strain the contents of the saucepan over the onion. Cover with plastic wrap and allow the mixture to cool for about 1½ hours.

for the lemon mustard dressing

Whisk the dressing ingredients together in a bowl and set aside.

Heat a charcoal grill, barbecue or chargrill pan until very hot. Season the mackerel with pink salt. Place the mackerel, skin side down, on the grill or barbecue and cook for 1 minute on each side.

Meanwhile, brush the bread with olive oil and chargrill until golden.

to serve

Remove the toasts from the grill, cut each piece into quarters, then brush with the garlic confit.

Cut each mackerel fillet into quarters and place a piece on top of each toast. Top with the pickled onion.

Grate the bottarga over the toasts and sprinkle with the chopped fennel fronds. Drizzle with the lemon mustard dressing and serve.

notes: Bottarga is a dry, salt-cured, pressed fish roe from the Mediterranean, in particular Sardinia and Sicily. It is often grated or thinly sliced before using; look for it in good fishmongers and specialty food stores.

Pickling spice — typically containing spices such as allspice, cloves, mustard seeds and peppercorns, among others — is a ready-made spice mix used for pickling vegetables and meats, sold in spice shops and fine grocers.

ingredients

5 small slimy or blue mackerel fillets
pink salt or sea salt, for sprinkling
5 slices bread (see Plain Bread recipe on page 25)
extra virgin olive oil, for brushing
12 Garlic Confit cloves (see recipe on page 208)
30 g (1 oz) bottarga (see notes)
2 tablespoons chopped fennel fronds and flowers (flowers optional)

pickled onions

100 ml (3½ fl oz) white wine vinegar
500 g (1 lb 2 oz) caster (superfine) sugar
30 g (1 oz) pickling spice (see notes)
1 cinnamon stick, broken
2 star anise, crushed
1 red chilli, split in half lengthways
1 onion, sliced very thinly using a mandoline

lemon mustard dressing

1½ tablespoons lemon juice
125 ml (4 fl oz/½ cup) extra virgin olive oil
2 teaspoons dijon mustard

LAVOSH

serves 6

ingredients

135 g (4¾ oz) plain (all-purpose) flour
1½ teaspoons poppy seeds
½ teaspoon caster (superfine) sugar
15 g (½ oz) butter, melted
60 ml (2 fl oz/¼ cup) milk, approximately
olive oil, for brushing
pink salt or sea salt, for sprinkling

method

Preheat the oven to 160°C (315°F/Gas 2–3).

Use your hands to combine the flour, poppy seeds, sugar and butter together in a mixing bowl. Add only as much of the milk as you need for the dough to come together. Cover the dough and chill in the fridge for 20 minutes.

Roll the dough out as thinly as possible into two sheets. Brush with olive oil and lightly sprinkle with pink salt.

Place on a large baking tray and bake for 10–12 minutes, or until golden brown. Remove from the oven and allow to cool on a wire rack.

Keep in an airtight container and break off shards as needed. The lavosh will keep for 3–4 days.

GARLIC FLATBREAD

makes 6

ingredients

550 g (1 lb 4 oz/3⅔ cups) plain (all-purpose) flour
140 ml (4½ fl oz) warm water
140 ml (4½ fl oz) milk
3 teaspoons (15 g/½ oz) instant dried yeast
1 quantity Garlic Confit cloves (see recipe on page 208)
1 tablespoon chopped parsley
1 tablespoon chopped rosemary
1 tablespoon chopped oregano
1 tablespoon chopped marjoram
200 ml (7 fl oz) extra virgin olive oil
pink salt or sea salt, for sprinkling

method

Place the flour and a good pinch of sea salt in the bowl of an electric mixer. Warm the water and milk slightly, add the yeast, then slowly add the mixture to the flour. Mix well on medium speed for at least 4–5 minutes.

Add the confit garlic cloves and fold them through, then rest the dough in a warm place for 10–15 minutes.

Divide the dough into six even portions, then roll out each portion with a rolling pin to about 5 mm (¼ inch) thick. Allow to prove again in a warm place for 10 minutes.

Mix the herbs and olive oil together in a bowl.

Heat a chargrill pan, barbecue or frying pan to medium-high and brush with a little oil.

Working in batches as needed, place the dough on the hot cooking surface brushed with a little oil. Cook for about 2 minutes, then turn over. Brush the cooked side with more herb oil mixture and cook for a further 2 minutes.

Sprinkle with pink salt and serve. This bread is best eaten the day it is baked.

PLAIN BREAD

method

Preheat the oven to 220°C (425°F/Gas 7).

Place all the ingredients in the bowl of an electric mixer. Begin kneading on low speed until the dough starts to come together. Now knead for 5–6 minutes on medium speed, until the dough is smooth and warm.

Turn the dough out onto a floured work surface and cut in half. Shape each portion into a ball.

Cover with a clean cloth and leave for about 10 minutes. After 10 minutes, knock the air out and roll into two loaves.

Place the loaves in a warm place with a cloth over them. Leave for about 1 hour, or until the loaves have doubled in size.

Score the loaves with a knife. Place on separate baking trays and bake for 10 minutes with steam. (If your oven doesn't have a steam setting, place a little water in a heatproof container in the bottom of the oven to create the steam.)

After 10 minutes, remove the water container, if using. Turn the oven down to 200°C (400°F/Gas 6) and bake for a further 10 minutes on dry heat.

Remove the loaves from the oven and allow to cool on wire racks.

This bread is best eaten the day it is baked.

ingredients

400 g (14 oz/2⅔ cups) plain (all-purpose) flour
1 teaspoon (4 g) instant dried yeast
1½ teaspoons sea salt
1 teaspoon caster (superfine) sugar
1 level teaspoon (4 g) bread improver
240 ml (8 fl oz) water

ZA'ATAR BREAD

makes 2 loaves

ingredients

400 g (14 oz/2⅔ cups) plain
    (all-purpose) flour
1 teaspoon (4 g) instant dried yeast
1½ teaspoons sea salt
2 teaspoons caster (superfine) sugar
1 tablespoon za'atar (see note)
1 level teaspoon (4 g) bread improver
130 ml (4½ fl oz) water
130 ml (4½ fl oz) milk
50 g (1¾ oz/¼ cup) sultanas
    (golden raisins)
extra virgin olive oil, for brushing

paste

1 tablespoon cornflour (cornstarch)
50 ml (1¾ fl oz) water
pink salt or sea salt, for sprinkling

method

Preheat the oven to 220°C (425°F/Gas 7).

Place all the bread ingredients, except the sultanas and olive oil, in the bowl of an electric mixer. Begin kneading on low speed until the dough starts to come together. Now knead for 5–6 minutes on medium speed, until the dough is smooth and warm. Add the sultanas and lightly mix through.

Turn the dough out onto a floured work surface and cut in half. Shape each portion into a ball, cover with a clean cloth and leave for about 10 minutes. After 10 minutes, knock the air out and roll the dough into two loaves.

Place the loaves in a warm place with a cloth over them. Leave for 1 hour, or until the loaves have doubled in size. Score the loaves with a knife.

for the paste

Mix the cornflour and water together until smooth. Brush the paste over the loaves, then sprinkle them with pink salt.

Place the loaves on separate baking trays and bake for 10 minutes with steam. (If your oven doesn't have a steam setting, place a little water in a heatproof container in the bottom of the oven to create the steam.)

After 10 minutes, remove the water container, if using. Turn the oven down to 200°C (400°F/Gas 6) and bake for a further 10 minutes on dry heat.

Remove the loaves from the oven and allow to cool on wire racks.

Before serving, brush the loaves with olive oil.

This bread is best eaten the day it is baked.

note: Also the name of a wild Middle Eastern herb, za'atar is a blend of spices including sumac, toasted sesame seeds, dried thyme and marjoram, commonly sprinkled over Middle Eastern meat and vegetable dishes, or mixed with salt and olive oil and used as a dip for bread. It is available from spice shops and fine food stores.

GINGER BREAD

makes 2 loaves

ingredients

200 g (7 oz) unsalted butter

400 g (14 oz) golden syrup or treacle

150 g (5½ oz/⅔ cup) caster (superfine) sugar

1 teaspoon orange marmalade

310 ml (10¾ fl oz/1¼ cups) milk

150 g (5½ oz/⅔ cup) grated fresh gingor

400 g (14 oz/2⅔ cups) plain (all-purpose) flour

1 teaspoon bicarbonate of soda (baking soda)

2 teaspoons baking powder

a pinch of sea salt

2 teaspoons mixed (pumpkin pie) spice

2 teaspoons Chinese five-spice

5 teaspoons ground ginger

4 free-range eggs

method

Preheat the oven to 160°C (315°F/Gas 2–3). Line two loaf (bar) tins, each measuring about 21 x 11 cm (8¼ x 4¼ inches) and 7 cm (2¾ inches) deep, with baking paper.

Melt the butter in a saucepan, then stir in the golden syrup, sugar, marmalade, milk and fresh ginger.

Sift the flour, bicarbonate of soda and baking powder into a bowl. Add the salt and spices and mix together.

Crack the eggs into a separate bowl and lightly whisk together. Add the eggs to the dry ingredients and mix together.

Add the melted butter mixture from the saucepan and continue to mix until well combined.

Divide the mixture between the two loaf tins. Transfer to the oven and bake for 1 hour.

Remove from the oven and allow the bread to rest in the tins for 5 minutes. Turn out onto wire racks to cool.

The ginger bread will keep for 1–2 days in an airtight container.

method

Pour the warm water into a small bowl, add the sugar and yeast and stir until dissolved. Set aside for 5–10 minutes, or until the mixture begins to foam. Blend in the warm milk, yoghurt and melted butter.

In a large mixing bowl, combine the flour, salt and baking powder. Pour in the yeast and milk mixture all at once and work it into the flour, using your hands.

Continue mixing, adding a little extra flour or water as needed, until the mixture leaves the side of the bowl. Knead for 6–8 minutes, or until smooth and elastic.

Place the dough in a lightly oiled bowl and turn to coat. Cover with a damp cloth and leave to stand in a warm place to rise for 4 hours, or until doubled in size.

Set an oven rack in the lower third of your oven. Place a large pizza pan or iron griddle on the oven rack. Preheat the oven to 285°C (545°F/Gas 10), or your oven's highest setting. Also preheat your oven grill (broiler) to its highest setting.

Punch the dough down and knead briefly. Divide into six pieces and shape them into balls. Place them on an oiled plate and cover with lightly oiled plastic wrap. Leave to rest for 10–15 minutes.

Roll out and stretch each ball until it is about 25 cm (10 inches) long and 13 cm (5 inches) wide. Remove the pizza pan from the oven, brush with olive oil and place one ball of dough on the pan. (If your pizza pan is big enough, you may be able to bake two naan breads at the one time.)

Bake for 4–5 minutes, or until the naan is puffed and has brown spots, then transfer to a wire rack, returning the pizza pan to the oven to keep it hot.

Place the bread under the grill until 'charcoal' dots appear on the surface. Wrap the finished bread in a clean cloth while baking the remaining naan.

Naan bread is best eaten the day it is baked.

ingredients

2 tablespoons warm water
1 teaspoon sugar
1½ teaspoons (7 g) instant dried yeast
60 ml (2 fl oz/¼ cup) warm milk
60 g (2¼ oz/¼ cup) plain yoghurt, at room temperature
80 ml (2½ fl oz/⅓ cup) melted unsalted butter
450 g (1 lb/3 cups) plain (all-purpose) flour
1 teaspoon sea salt
½ teaspoon baking powder
extra virgin olive oil, for brushing

BRIOCHE

method

Preheat the oven to 200°C (400°F/Gas 6).

Place the flour, yeast, salt and sugar in the bowl of an electric mixer and mix on low to medium speed to combine. Add the egg, egg yolk and milk and continue to combine until the mixture forms a dough.

When the dough pulls away from the side of the bowl, add half the butter and mix until the lumps have dissolved. Repeat with the remaining butter. Continue mixing until the dough has a smooth, shiny consistency.

Leave the dough in the mixing bowl and cover with a clean cloth. Leave in a warm place for 1 hour, or until the dough has doubled in size.

Remove the dough from the bowl and place in a non-stick loaf (bar) tin, measuring about 21 x 11 cm (8¼ x 4¼ inches) and 7 cm (2¾ inches) deep.

Cover with foil and leave to rise for a further 20–25 minutes.

Transfer to the oven and bake for 20 minutes. Remove the foil and bake for a further 10–20 minutes, or until golden brown. Remove from the oven and leave the brioche in the tin for 5–8 minutes.

Turn out onto a wire rack to cool before serving.

The brioche will keep in an airtight container for 2–3 days.

ingredients

290 g (10¼ oz) strong baker's flour
1 teaspoon (5 g) instant dried yeast
a pinch of sea salt
5 teaspoons (25 g) caster (superfine) sugar
1 free-range egg, plus 1 free-range egg yolk
60 ml (2 fl oz/¼ cup) cold milk
150 g (5½ oz) butter, at room temperature

There's a saying in the food world that you can always judge the quality of a chef from the soup or stock they can produce. This saying has always stuck in my mind, and I believe it to be pretty true.

You can't beat a perfect soup or broth, so I've included some simple soup recipes in this chapter, as well as some that require a little more time to prepare, such as my Crab & Chargrilled Corn Soup (page 78) and Coconut Broth (page 79).

Also featured in this chapter is a great selection of starters, including salads, seafood dishes and vegetarian offerings that are perfect for dinner parties, or even as light meals on their own.

These dishes focus on using fresh, good-quality ingredients so you don't need to spend hours in the kitchen to create something wonderful.

My favourite dishes include the Waldorf Salad with Bresaola (page 63), and Barbecued Prawns with Avocado & Mango Salsa (page 34) — so perfect for summer.

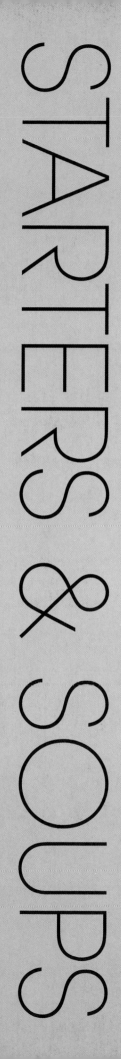

STARTERS & SOUPS

BARBECUED PRAWNS WITH AVOCADO & MANGO SALSA

serves 4

ingredients

16 raw king prawns (shrimp), peeled
    and deveined, tails left intact
extra virgin olive oil, for drizzling
¼ iceberg lettuce, thinly sliced
1 avocado, diced
Vietnamese mint leaves, to garnish

mango salsa

2 ripe mangoes
¼ red onion, very finely diced
1 red chilli, seeded and finely chopped
2 tablespoons roughly chopped
    Vietnamese mint
2 tablespoons roughly chopped
    coriander (cilantro) leaves
1½ tablespoons chardonnay vinegar
    or white wine vinegar
1 tablespoon extra virgin olive oil

for the mango salsa

Peel the mangoes, then cut off the cheeks and as much flesh off the stones as possible. Dice the mango flesh and place in a mixing bowl.

Add the remaining salsa ingredients, season with sea salt and freshly ground black pepper and mix lightly.

for the prawns

Place the prawns on a tray. Season and drizzle with just enough olive oil to coat the prawns.

Place the prawns on a hot barbecue or frying pan and cook for 2 minutes on one side.

Turn the prawns over and cook for a further 2 minutes. Remove and rest on a plate for another 2 minutes.

to serve

Add the lettuce to the mango salsa and place on a platter or four individual serving plates. Scatter the prawns and avocado on top.

Garnish with Vietnamese mint, drizzle with a little more olive oil and serve.

BARBECUED PRAWNS WITH WITLOF, RAISIN & PARSLEY SALAD

serves 4

ingredients
4 witlof (chicory), outer layer removed
50 g (1¾ oz) butter, plus extra for
    pan-frying
1 tablespoon sugar
200 ml (7 fl oz) Veal Stock (see recipe
    on page 195)
12 raw king prawns (shrimp),
    peeled and deveined, tails left intact
½ cup flat-leaf (Italian) parsley leaves
150 g (5½ oz) raisins
25 ml (¾ fl oz) balsamic vinegar
extra virgin olive oil, for drizzling

method
Cut each witlof in half lengthways.

Combine the butter and sugar in a frying pan over high heat, to make a light caramel.

Place the witlof halves in the pan and brown on each side for 1 minute.

Pour in the stock and continue to cook the witlof for 3 minutes, or until tender.

Meanwhile, place the prawns in a separate frying pan and sauté in a little extra butter for about 2 minutes on each side, or until golden brown and crispy.

to serve
Place the caramelised witlof in the centre of four serving plates and drizzle with the remaining pan juices.

Toss the parsley, raisins and prawns together with the vinegar and a drizzle of olive oil. Season the salad with sea salt and freshly ground black pepper.

Pile the salad on top of the witlof, trying to get as much height as possible. Serve warm.

MUSSEL TORTELLINI WITH CORN PURÉE & SAUCE VIERGE

serves 6

for the corn purée

Melt the butter in a large saucepan. Add the shallot and sauté for 2–3 minutes over medium heat. Add the capsicum and corn kernels, then cover and cook for 6–8 minutes. Stir in the cream, reduce the heat to medium–low, then cover and cook for a further 25 minutes.

Transfer the mixture to a food processor and blend until smooth. Pass through a fine sieve and set aside.

for the mussel tortellini

Cook the corn cob in a saucepan of simmering water for 5 minutes. Remove the corn and place in iced water until cool enough to handle. Cut the kernels off the cob, then place in a bowl. Add the mussel meat and coriander and season with sea salt and freshly ground black pepper.

Place a spoonful of the mussel mixture on each gow gee wrapper and lightly wet one edge of the wrapper with a little water.

Fold each wrapper in half, so they resemble half-moons. Now fold the wrapper into a ring, so that the two edges on the flat side overlap. Stick them down with a little more water. Place the tortellini on a lightly floured tray.

for the sauce vierge

Heat the stock in a saucepan. Add the olive oil and remove from the heat. Stir in the lemon juice and capers and season to taste. Set aside.

Place a saucepan of water on the stove, add a little sea salt and bring to a simmer. Gently add the tortellini in two batches and cook each batch for 4–5 minutes. Remove from the water using a slotted spoon and place on a tray. Season to taste.

to serve

Gently reheat the corn purée, checking the seasoning, then place small dollops around six serving plates. Place the tortellini on top.

Mix the parsley through the sauce vierge and drizzle over the tortellini. Garnish with the chervil and serve.

corn purée

1 tablespoon butter
2 French shallots, finely chopped
1 yellow capsicum (pepper), chopped
425 g (15 oz) tin corn kernels, drained
200 ml (7 fl oz) thin (pouring) cream

mussel tortellini

1 corn cob
250 g (9 oz) mussel meat, roughly chopped
½ cup coriander (cilantro) leaves
18 gow gee (egg) dumpling wrappers
plain (all-purpose) flour, for dusting
3 tablespoons chervil leaves

sauce vierge

50 ml (1¾ fl oz) Fish Stock (see recipe on page 196)
50 ml (1¾ fl oz) extra virgin olive oil
1 tablespoon lemon juice
2 teaspoons capers
2 teaspoons chopped flat-leaf (Italian) parsley

BABY VEGETABLE & GOAT'S CURD SALAD

serves 4

method

Preheat the oven to 70–80°C (150–175°F/Gas ¼). Place the olives on a baking tray and into the oven. Place a clean cloth on the oven door to ensure that when it closes there is a space where steam can escape. Leave the olives for 4–5 hours, or until dehydrated. Remove from the oven and leave to cool.

Heat the oven to 180°C (350°F/Gas 4). Wash the turnips and carrots and place in a roasting tin. Drizzle with olive oil and season with sea salt and freshly ground black pepper. Roast for 20–25 minutes, or until the turnips and carrots are tender, taking care not to overcook them.

Place the yellow and red beetroot in two separate saucepans and cover with water, adding 50 ml (1¾ fl oz) of the vinegar to each pan. Cook for 15 minutes, or until the beetroot are soft in the centre when pierced with a sharp knife. Strain and set aside to cool slightly before rubbing off the skin with a clean cloth. Set aside.

Add half the ghee to a frying pan and melt over medium-low heat. Add the ginger bread croutons and cook for 3–5 minutes, or until crisp and golden, tossing frequently. Drain on paper towels and season with a little sea salt.

Wipe the pan out with a paper towel and place back over medium heat. Add the remaining ghee, then sauté the asparagus for a couple of minutes, or until just tender. Drain on paper towels and season to taste.

to serve

Place all the cooked vegetables on a tray and drizzle with a little honey thyme dressing. Season to taste.

Dollop the goat's curd onto four serving plates. Arrange the vegetables, ginger bread croutons, rocket and dried black olives over the top.

Drizzle each plate with a little more honey thyme dressing and serve.

ingredients

55 g (2 oz/⅓ cup) pitted kalamata olives
8 baby turnips
8 baby heirloom carrots
extra virgin olive oil, for drizzling
12 baby yellow beetroot (beets)
8 baby red beetroot (beets)
100 ml (3½ fl oz) cabernet sauvignon vinegar or red wine vinegar
4 tablespoons ghee (clarified butter)
2 slices Ginger Bread (see recipe on page 28), cut into croutons
12 asparagus spears, peeled
Honey Thyme Dressing (see recipe on page 201), to serve
4 tablespoons fresh goat's curd
45 g (1½ oz/1 cup) baby rocket (arugula)

TEMPURA PRAWNS WITH MISO MAYO & CARROT & DAIKON SALAD

serves 4

ingredients
12 large raw prawns (shrimp)
½ quantity Miso Mayo (see recipe
    on page 207)
baby watercress leaves, to garnish

carrot and daikon salad
½ carrot
¼ medium-sized daikon radish
30 g (1 oz) unsalted butter
2½ tablespoons honey
1 tablespoon toasted sesame seeds
    (see Crab Omelette recipe on
    page 46)

tempura batter
vegetable oil, for deep-frying
150 g (5½ oz) rice flour, plus extra
    for dusting the prawns
150 g (5½ oz) tapioca flour
2 ice cubes
juice of 1 lime
juice of 1 lemon
250 ml (9 fl oz/1 cup) soda water

for the prawns
Peel the prawns, leaving the heads and tails attached. Cut away the intestinal vein using a sharp knife, then insert a skewer lengthways through the middle of each prawn.

for the carrot and daikon salad
Peel the carrot and daikon to remove the outer skin. Peel the carrot and daikon into strips, until you reach the core. Discard the cores.

Heat the butter and honey in a frying pan until the butter froths. Add the vegetable strips and quickly cook over medium heat until softened.

Remove from the heat, season with sea salt and freshly ground black pepper and add the sesame seeds. Place in a bowl and cover with plastic wrap to keep warm.

for the tempura batter
Fill a deep-fryer or large heavy-based saucepan one-third full of vegetable oil and heat the oil to 170°C (325°F), or until a cube of bread dropped into the oil turns golden brown in 20 seconds.

Meanwhile, place the rice flour and tapioca flour in a bowl. Add the ice, lime juice, lemon juice and soda water and mix with a fork to form a batter — a few little lumps are fine as they will crisp up in the deep-fryer.

When the oil is ready, lightly flour the prawns in the rice flour, dusting off any excess. Lightly coat the prawns in the batter.

Very slowly add half the prawns to the deep-fryer, to avoid any hot oil splashes. Cook for 4–5 minutes, or until the batter is golden and the prawns are just cooked through.

Remove using a slotted spoon and briefly drain on paper towels.

Reheat the oil and cook the remaining prawns in the same way. Season the prawns and remove the skewers.

to serve
Place a dollop of miso mayo on four serving plates. Pile a little carrot and daikon salad on the side of each plate and garnish with watercress leaves. Lay three prawns on each plate and serve.

PAN-FRIED POTATO GNOCCHI WITH SUMMER VEGETABLES

for the gnocchi

Preheat the oven to 180°C (350°F/Gas 4).

Sprinkle the rock salt over a baking tray and place the potatoes on top. (The salt helps dry the potatoes out, for a better gnocchi.) Bake for 1–1½ hours, or until the potatoes are soft in the centre when tested with a sharp knife.

Allow the potatoes to cool for 5 minutes. Cut in half, scoop out the flesh, then squeeze the flesh through a mouli or potato ricer, into a large bowl.

Add the flour, nutmeg, egg and egg white. Season with sea salt and freshly ground black pepper, and mix together into a dough, taking care not to overwork it. Shape the dough into a ball and place on a floured work surface.

Roll fist-sized pieces of the dough into thin snake-like shapes. Cut into little 'pillows' and place on floured trays.

Bring a pot of salted water to the boil. Add half the gnocchi, allow them to rise to the top, then cook for a further 1–2 minutes. Remove with a slotted spoon and place in ice-cold water to cool. Repeat with the remaining gnocchi.

Remove the gnocchi from the ice water and place on a clean cloth. Gently pat dry and set aside.

Cook the corn cobs in a pot of salted boiling water for 10 minutes. Remove with a slotted spoon and refresh in iced water, keeping the pot of water simmering on the stove.

Pat the corn cobs dry and place on a chopping board. Using a sharp knife, slice off the kernels. Set aside in a bowl.

Place a non-stick frying pan over medium heat. Drizzle the hot pan with olive oil and add the gnocchi (you may need to work in two batches, depending on your pan size). Fry the gnocchi for 2 minutes on each side, until golden. Add the butter and allow to foam without burning.

Meanwhile, cook the asparagus and zucchini in the pot of simmering water for 2 minutes. Remove with a slotted spoon.

Add the asparagus, zucchini, corn kernels and lemon thyme to the same frying pan as the gnocchi and continue to cook for 2 minutes, or until all the ingredients are tender.

Strain the mixture through a sieve and season to taste. Place on a tray and toss the parmesan and a little of the truffle verjuice dressing through.

Divide among eight serving plates. Garnish with the micro greens, drizzle with more truffle verjuice dressing and serve.

ingredients

2 corn cobs
16 young asparagus spears
2 zucchini (courgettes), cut into 1.5 cm
   (⅝ inch) squares
2 teaspoons lemon thyme leaves
80 g (2¾ oz/¾ cup) finely grated
   parmesan cheese
250 ml (9 fl oz/1 cup) Truffle Verjuice
   Dressing (see recipe on page 202)
micro greens, to garnish

gnocchi

1.25 kg (2 lb 12 oz/4 cups) rock salt
400 g (14 oz) desiree potatoes
160 g (5½ oz/heaped 1 cup) plain
   (all-purpose) flour
a pinch of freshly grated nutmeg
1 free-range egg, lightly beaten
1 free-range egg white, lightly beaten
olive oil, for drizzling
125 g (4½ oz) butter

GRILLED SARDINE & HALOUMI PANZANELLA

serves 6

ingredients

2 red capsicums (peppers)
extra virgin olive oil, for drizzling
2 vine-ripened tomatoes, sliced
125 g (4½ oz) heirloom cherry
   tomatoes, halved
3 French shallots, sliced
48 croutons (see Caesar Salad recipe
   on page 62)
½ red chilli, chopped
12 white anchovies (see note on
   page 10)
12 basil leaves
6 slices haloumi cheese, each 1 cm
   (½ inch) thick
6 fresh sardines, butterflied

dressing

50 ml (1¾ fl oz) aged balsamic
   vinegar
150 ml (5 fl oz) extra virgin olive oil

method

Preheat the oven to 200°C (400°F/Gas 6).

Place the capsicums on a baking tray, drizzle with olive oil and season with sea salt and freshly ground black pepper. Roast for 20 minutes, or until the skins have blistered.

Place the capsicums in a bowl, cover with plastic wrap and allow to sweat in their skins for 30 minutes. Remove the seeds and membranes from the capsicums, then peel the skin away — it should slip off very easily. Dice the flesh into largish pieces and place in a mixing bowl.

Add the tomatoes, shallot, croutons, chilli, anchovies and basil. Set aside.

Dress the haloumi and sardines separately with a little olive oil. Season the sardines.

Heat a frying pan, chargrill pan or barbecue. Cook the haloumi over medium heat for 1–1½ minutes on each side, or until golden. Remove to a tray.

Cook the sardines, skin side down, with a little more oil for 1½–2 minutes, or until just cooked through, then add to the haloumi.

for the dressing

Mix together the dressing ingredients, then toss half the dressing through the salad. Season to taste.

to serve

Divide the salad among six serving plates. Cut the haloumi in half, diagonally and widthways, then arrange on top of each salad.

Cut each sardine lengthways into two fillets, and arrange two fillets over each salad. Drizzle with the remaining dressing and serve.

SEARED SCALLOPS WITH BABY BEETROOT, BUFFALO MOZZARELLA & HONEY THYME DRESSING

serves 4

method

Preheat the oven to 180°C (350°F/Gas 4).

Place the red and yellow beetroot on separate trays lined with foil and drizzle with olive oil. Add the thyme and season with sea salt and freshly ground black pepper. Wrap the foil around the beetroot and bake for 30 minutes, or until the beetroot are soft in the centre when tested with a sharp knife.

Half-fill a saucepan with water and add a little sea salt. Bring to a simmer, add the asparagus and blanch for 2 minutes. Remove and cool in an iced water bath, then drain on paper towels and set aside.

Mix all the herbs together in a bowl, lightly tearing them with your hands.

Heat a little olive oil in a frying pan over high heat. When the frying pan is hot, add the scallops and cook until they are just turning white, turning them once. The scallops will take less than a couple of minutes, so take care not to overcook them. Drain on paper towels.

Peel and slice the beetroots, place on four serving plates and season to taste. Add a mozzarella half to each plate, then scatter the herbs over.

Arrange four scallops around each plate. Drizzle with the honey thyme dressing and serve.

ingredients

12 baby red beetroot (beets)
12 baby yellow beetroot (beets)
extra virgin olive oil, for drizzling
    and pan-frying
5 thyme sprigs
12 green asparagus spears
10 chives, cut into batons
20 mint leaves
30 tarragon leaves
20 coriander (cilantro) leaves
20 parsley leaves
16 sea scallops
2 buffalo mozzarella cheeses, halved
125 ml (4 fl oz/½ cup) Honey Thyme
    Dressing (see recipe on page 201)

CRAB OMELETTE, ENOKI MUSHROOM SALAD & MISO BROTH

makes 1 omelette

enoki mushroom salad
2 teaspoons sesame seeds
2 basil leaves
4 mint leaves
8 coriander (cilantro) leaves
10 enoki mushrooms, separated
¼ mild red chilli, seeded and julienned
2 teaspoons Crisp Shallots
    (see recipe on page 206)

fish sauce dressing
1 tablespoon extra virgin olive oil
juice of ½ lime
1 teaspoon fish sauce

omelette
50 g (1¾ oz) blue swimmer crab
    meat, picked
1½ tablespoons Miso Mayo
    (see recipe on page 207)
3 free-range eggs
2 tablespoons butter
50 ml (1¾ fl oz) Miso Broth
    (see recipe on page 203)

for the enoki mushroom salad
Warm a frying pan over medium–low heat. Add the sesame seeds, stirring them around in the pan. Cook for 2 minutes, or until they are golden in colour. Remove from the pan and place on a paper towel to cool.

Place the sesame seeds in a small mixing bowl with the basil, mint, coriander, mushrooms, chilli and crisp shallots. Set aside.

for the fish sauce dressing
Combine the dressing ingredients in a small bowl. Cover and set aside.

for the omelette
Preheat the oven to 170°C (325°F/Gas 3). Place the crabmeat on a baking tray and coat with the miso mayo. Transfer to the oven to warm through for about 2–3 minutes.

Beat the eggs in a bowl until combined.

Heat a heavy-based non-stick frying pan over medium heat and melt the butter.

Meanwhile, heat the miso broth in a small saucepan, removing it from the heat just before it comes to the boil.

When the butter in the pan is hot enough — a drop of water should hiss when added to it — pour in the eggs. Stir for 10 seconds, then flatten the mixture out around the pan. Allow the eggs to cook for up to 1 minute, or until the bottom starts to set.

With a rubber spatula, gently push one edge of the egg into the centre of the pan, while tilting the pan to allow the liquid egg to flow in underneath.

Repeat with the other edges, until there is only a little soft liquid remaining. The eggs should now resemble a bright yellow pancake, which should easily slide around on the non-stick surface. If it is sticking to the pan, loosen it with your spatula.

Place the warmed crabmeat in the middle of the omelette.

With your spatula, lift one edge of the egg and fold it across and over, so that the omelette edges line up. Gently transfer the finished omelette to a serving plate-bowl.

Toss the dressing through the herb salad and arrange over the omelette. Drizzle with the hot miso broth and serve.

CARROT, RICOTTA, SAGE & SESAME RAVIOLI WITH BURNT BUTTER & AMARETTI CRUMBS

serves 4

ingredients
1 quantity Pasta Dough (see recipe on page 207)
plain (all-purpose) flour, for dusting
1 free-range egg, beaten
2 tablespoons toasted pine nuts
2 tablespoons currants, soaked in port
    for at least 30 minutes
2 Amaretti Biscuits (see recipe on page 173),
    crushed

carrot and ricotta filling
100 ml (3½ fl oz) extra virgin olive oil
200 g (7 oz) unsalted butter

5 garlic cloves, thinly sliced
16 sage leaves
500 g (1 lb 2 oz) carrots, sliced
200 g (7 oz) ricotta
150 g (5½ oz/1½ cups) grated parmesan cheese
40 g (1½ oz/¼ cup) toasted sesame seeds
    (see Crab Omelette recipe on page 46)
pink salt or sea salt, to season

burnt butter dressing
200 g (7 oz) unsalted butter
16 sage leaves
juice of ½ lemon

for the carrot and ricotta filling
Heat the olive oil and butter in a large saucepan over medium heat and begin frying off the garlic and sage leaves. Add the carrot, then cover and cook for 15 minutes, or until very tender.

Transfer the mixture to a food processor and pulse until you have a slightly rough mix. Scrape into a bowl, cover with baking paper and leave to cool to room temperature.

Once cooled, add the ricotta, parmesan and sesame seeds. Season with pink salt and freshly ground black pepper and mix together. Cover and set aside.

for the ravioli
Divide the dough into five even pieces then roll through a pasta roller until the sheets are about 2 mm (¹⁄₁₆ inch) thick. Set aside on a tray, lightly flouring between the sheets. Cover with a damp cloth and place in the refrigerator so they don't dry out.

Lay two pasta sheets on a lightly floured work surface. One sheet will be the bottom half of the ravioli, and the other sheet will be the top. Keep the remaining layers covered while you are making the ravioli.

Place tablespoons of the carrot mixture on the bottom pasta sheet, leaving a good space in between each. Using a pastry brush, brush the beaten egg around the filling, then thinly coat the entire surface of the pasta sheets.

Seal the two pasta sheets together by gently laying the top sheet of pasta over the bottom sheet, ensuring that the two sheets match up evenly. Work out any air bubbles, by gently but firmly pushing the air from the filling to the edge of the pasta with your fingers. Continue pushing the air out until there are no more air bubbles trapped in the ravioli — trapped air will expand during cooking, causing the ravioli to burst. Repeat with the remaining pasta sheets and filling.

Place the dull side of a pastry cutter around the filling mounds, and press down lightly to shape the ravioli, ensuring you don't cut through the pasta dough. Cut the dough into squares using a sharp knife.

Three-quarters fill a large saucepan with water. Add a pinch of salt and bring to a gentle simmer. Gently add the ravioli in two batches and cook each batch for 4–5 minutes.

for the burnt butter dressing
While the ravioli are cooking, place a large frying pan over medium heat. Add the butter and sage leaves and cook for 3 minutes, or until the butter begins to foam and turns a nutty brown colour.

Add the lemon juice, remove from the heat and season to taste.

When the ravioli are cooked, remove them from the saucepan with a slotted spoon and transfer to a bowl. Using a spoon, gently mix the burnt butter sauce through, reserving the sage leaves.

Divide the ravioli among four serving plates and drizzle with any remaining burnt butter sauce from the bowl.

Sprinkle with the sage leaves from the sauce, pine nuts and currants, scatter the amaretto crumbs over and serve.

SMOKED SALMON & POTATO TERRINE

serves 8–10

terrine

12 desiree potatoes, all medium size
2 litres (70 fl oz/8 cups) thin (pouring) cream
4 garlic cloves
1 thyme sprig
250 g (9 oz) cream cheese
½ cup dill, chopped
1 side of a 1.2 kg (2 lb 10 oz) smoked salmon, sliced

salad

12 baby red beetroot (beets)
12 baby yellow beetroot (beets)
100 ml (3½ fl oz) red wine vinegar
1 teaspoon finely chopped dill
1 cup mixed baby herb leaves

red wine vinaigrette

50 ml (1¾ fl oz) red wine vinegar
150 ml (5 fl oz) extra virgin olive oil

to serve

Brioche, sliced and toasted (see recipe on page 31), to serve

for the terrine

Peel the potatoes and cut them into rectangles. Thinly slice using a mandoline.

Place the potato slices in a saucepan and cover with the cream. Add the garlic and thyme, season with sea salt and freshly ground black pepper, then bring to a simmer. Cook for 8–10 minutes, or until tender.

Lightly drain the potatoes, reserving the cream and leaving a thin coat of cream over them.

Whisk the cream cheese, dill and 150 ml (5 fl oz) of the cream until smooth, then season to taste.

Line a 28 cm (11¼ inch) terrine mould with plastic wrap, making sure that there is enough on each side to cover the top of the finished terrine.

To build the terrine, layer the bottom of the mould with the potato slices. Brush with the cream cheese mixture, then add a layer of smoked salmon.

Continue repeating the layers until the ingredients reach the top of the terrine, finishing with a layer of potato.

Fold the sides of the plastic wrap over the top of the terrine, ensuring that it is completely covered.

Place in the refrigerator overnight, with a heavy object on top to ensure it is pressed down.

for the salad

Place the red and yellow beetroot in two separate saucepans and cover with water, adding 50 ml (1¾ fl oz) of the vinegar to each saucepan.

Cook for 15 minutes, or until the beetroot are soft in the centre when pierced with a sharp knife. Strain and leave to cool slightly before rubbing off the skin with a clean cloth.

Place the beetroot in a large bowl with the dill and baby herb leaves and gently mix together.

for the red wine vinaigrette

Combine the vinegar and olive oil and set aside.

to serve

Turn the terrine out of the mould, onto a clean chopping board. Cut the terrine into eight to ten slices.

Drizzle the vinaigrette over the salad and serve with the terrine, with slices of toasted brioche on the side.

QUAIL WITH ZUCCHINI, BASIL, PINE NUTS & CURRANTS

serves 4

method

Rub the quails with a mixture of the thyme, lemon zest and enough olive oil to ensure the marinade coats the birds. Marinate for at least 1 hour in the refrigerator.

Melt the butter and heat a little olive oil in a frying pan over medium heat. Gently cook the zucchini for 3 minutes, or until softened. Stir in the currants, pine nuts and two-thirds of the basil. Season with pink salt and freshly ground black pepper and keep warm.

Drain most of the marinade from the quails and season the birds lightly.

Heat a barbecue or a chargrill pan until very hot. Place the quails on the grill, skin side down. Cook for 2–3 minutes, then turn and cook the other side for another 2 minutes.

Place the birds on a tray and rest for 3 minutes.

to serve

Place a mound of the zucchini mixture on four serving plates. Cut the quails in half and sit two halves on top.

Drizzle with a little more olive oil, garnish with the remaining basil and serve.

ingredients

4 quails, boned, leaving the wings
  and drumsticks attached
10 thyme sprigs
zest of 1 lemon
extra virgin olive oil, for drizzling and
  pan-frying
50 g (1¾ oz) unsalted butter
4 small zucchini (courgettes), grated
3 tablespoons currants, soaked in port
  for at least 30 minutes
2 tablespoons lightly toasted pine nuts
20 basil leaves, chopped
pink salt or sea salt, to season

MICHEL ROUX'S ONION TARTS WITH SOFT POACHED EGG & ASPARAGUS

serves 4

ingredients

100 g (3½ oz) butter

2 large onions, about 500 g (1 lb 2 oz) in total, thinly sliced

150 ml (5 fl oz) thick (double) cream

a few thyme leaves, plus extra to garnish

2 ready-made puff pastry or flan pastry sheets

plain (all-purpose) flour, for dusting

12 green asparagus spears, peeled if thick

extra virgin olive oil, for pan-frying

1 quantity Honey Thyme Dressing (see recipe on page 201)

100 g (3½ oz/1¼ cups) shaved parmesan cheese

poached eggs

4 small free-range eggs

60 ml (2 fl oz/¼ cup) white wine vinegar

1 teaspoon sea salt

method

Melt the butter in a heavy-based saucepan over low heat. Gently cook the onion for 45 minutes, stirring every 10 minutes.

Stir in the cream, add the thyme leaves and simmer for another 20 minutes. Season with sea salt and freshly ground black pepper, transfer to a bowl and set aside.

To make the tarts, roll out the pastry on a lightly floured work surface to a 3 mm (⅛ inch) thickness. Using a 12 cm (4½ inch) plain round pastry cutter, cut out four pastry discs. Place on a sheet of baking paper and chill for 20 minutes.

Meanwhile, preheat the oven to 170°C (325°F/Gas 3).

Transfer the pastry discs, still on their sheet of baking paper, to a baking tray. Prick each pastry disc four or five times with a fork, then spread the caramelised onion evenly over the top. Bake for 25–30 minutes, or until the bottom of the pastry is well cooked and crisp.

for the poached eggs

While the pastry is baking, poach the eggs. Fill a wide saucepan with about 8 cm (3¼ inches) water, add the vinegar and salt and bring to the boil over medium–high heat.

Reduce the heat to medium–low — the water should be just simmering, with small bubbles rising from the base of the pan, and small ripples across the top of the water.

Using a wooden spoon or whisk, stir the simmering water in one direction to create a whirlpool; this will help give your poached eggs a neat shape.

Crack an egg onto a saucer. Slide the egg from the saucer as close to the water as possible, into the centre of the whirlpool. Cook, without stirring, for 2–3 minutes for a semi-soft yolk, or 3–4 minutes for a firm-set yolk.

Using a slotted spoon, transfer the egg to paper towels to drain. Season to taste and keep warm.

Repeat the process with the remaining eggs, cooking them one at a time.

Meanwhile, place another saucepan over medium heat and cook the asparagus in a little olive oil for 2 minutes, or until tender. Transfer to a plate and keep warm.

to serve

Place a poached egg on each onion tart, along with three asparagus spears. Drizzle with the honey thyme dressing and top with the parmesan. Garnish with extra thyme leaves and serve on four warm plates.

SEARED SPICED TUNA WITH CELERIAC & APPLE REMOULADE

serves 4

method

Season the tuna with sea salt and freshly ground black pepper, then roll in the cajun spice mix.

Place a frying pan over very high heat. Carefully add a little olive oil to the pan. Sear the tuna on each side for no longer than 10 seconds.

Place the tuna on a tray, then cool in the refrigerator for 5 minutes to stop the cooking process and to make it easier to cut. Transfer the cooled tuna to a chopping board, then cut each block into five slices.

Cover and set aside at room temperature.

for the celeriac and apple remoulade

Place the celeriac in a bowl and sprinkle with the salt. Leave to cure for 10 minutes, then rinse the salt off and drain the celeriac. Pat dry with paper towels and place in a bowl with the apple and sorrel.

In a separate bowl, mix together the crème fraîche, sour cream, capers, lemon juice and mustard. Drizzle over the celeriac mixture and mix well.

to serve

Place small mounds of the remoulade around four serving plates, then add the tuna.

Remove the seeds from the bush lime and squeeze the juice over and around the tuna. Garnish with chervil sprigs, drizzle with a little olive oil and serve.

ingredients

400 g (14 oz) sashimi-grade tuna, cut into 4 blocks
2 tablespoons cajun spice mix
extra virgin olive oil, for pan-frying and drizzling
1 native bush lime or regular lime, halved
chervil sprigs, to garnish

celeriac and apple remoulade

¼ celeriac, peeled and julienned
2 teaspoons fine sea salt
½ green apple, julienned
2 sorrel leaves, julienned
2 tablespoons crème fraîche
2 tablespoons sour cream
1 tablespoon salted capers, soaked in water to remove excess salt
juice of ½ lemon
2 teaspoons dijon mustard

SEARED SCALLOPS WITH BLUE CHEESE POLENTA, SHIITAKE MUSHROOMS & TRUFFLE OIL

serves 4

ingredients

8 fresh shiitake mushrooms
1½ cups wild rocket (arugula), washed
2 tablespoons extra virgin olive oil
12 medium to large sea scallops, roe removed
truffle oil, for drizzling (optional)

polenta

900 ml (31 fl oz) milk
200 g (7 oz) instant polenta
50 ml (1¾ fl oz) thin (pouring) cream
100 g (3½ oz) good-quality blue cheese, such as stilton

method

Thinly slice the mushrooms. Add them to a saucepan of salted boiling water and blanch for about 30 seconds. Drain well, then toss in a bowl with the rocket.

for the polenta

Pour the milk into a saucepan, add a pinch of sea salt and bring to the boil. Pour in the polenta in a gradual steady stream, stirring constantly. Cook over low heat for 5 minutes.

Stir in the cream, then crumble in the blue cheese and stir until melted through.

Just before the polenta is ready, heat a heavy-based frying pan over high heat and add the olive oil. When the oil is hot, add the scallops and cook until they are just turning white, turning them once. The scallops will take less than a couple of minutes, so take care not to overcook them.

to serve

Spoon the polenta into the middle of four serving plate-bowls, then flatten the mounds out a little with a knife.

Arrange three scallops around each polenta mound. Top with a small pile of the rocket and mushrooms.

Serve warm, drizzled with a little truffle oil if desired.

CAESAR SALAD

serves 4

ingredients

4 thin slices Plain Bread (see recipe
    on page 25) or white bread, torn
extra virgin olive oil, for drizzling
4 bacon rashers, rind removed,
    coarsely chopped
3 baby cos (romaine) lettuce,
    hearts left whole
60 g (2¼ oz/⅔ cup) shaved parmesan
    cheese
4 warm poached free-range eggs
    (see Michel Roux's Onion Tarts
    recipe on page 56)

dressing

1½ tablespoons dijon mustard
1 garlic clove, finely chopped
2 teaspoons worcestershire sauce
1½ tablespoons chardonnay vinegar
100 ml (3½ fl oz) verjuice (see note on
    page 202), approximately
4 anchovies, finely chopped (optional)
200 ml (7 fl oz) vegetable oil
a splash of Tabasco sauce

method

Preheat the oven to 180°C (350°F/Gas 4).
    Spread the bread in a single layer on a baking tray
and drizzle with olive oil. Bake for 10–15 minutes, or until the
croutons are crisp and golden. Set aside to cool completely.

for the dressing

Place the mustard, garlic, worcestershire sauce, vinegar and
half the verjuice in a food processor. Add the anchovies,
if using, and blend to combine.
    With the motor running, add the vegetable oil in a thin
steady stream until the dressing is thick, then add a little of the
remaining verjuice until the dressing is a pourable consistency.
Season with sea salt, freshly ground black pepper and Tabasco
sauce and set aside.

Heat a non-stick frying pan over medium heat and cook the
bacon, stirring often, for 3–4 minutes, or until crisp and browned.
Transfer to a plate lined with paper towels.

to serve

Arrange the lettuce, croutons, bacon and half the parmesan
on a serving platter.
    Drizzle the dressing over, top with the poached eggs
and remaining parmesan and serve.

WALDORF SALAD WITH BRESAOLA

method

Place the apple slices in a bowl. Wash the celery and cut into batons, then add to the bowl with the celery leaves.

Slice a small piece off the bottom of each witlof and pull off the leaves. Rinse the leaves, then dry them using a salad spinner. Add the witlof to the bowl with the walnuts.

Drizzle the salad with a little walnut oil and season with sea salt and freshly ground black pepper.

for the dressing

Whisk all the dressing ingredients together in a bowl. Add the dressing to the salad bowl and mix through.

to serve

Divide half the salad and half the bresaola among four serving plates. Add another layer of the salad and top with the remaining bresaola.

Drizzle with a little more walnut oil and serve.

note: Originating in Italy, bresaola is a prime beef portion that has been cured by rubbing with salt and a mixture of spices, then air-dried for several months, until hard and purplish red. It is generally served thinly sliced as part of an antipasto platter. Wagyu bresaola, made from wagyu beef, is available from specialist butchers.

ingredients

1 red apple, cored and sliced
1 green apple, cored and sliced
2 celery stalks (close to the heart is sweetest), plus 20 yellow celery leaves (from close to the heart)
2 red witlof (chicory)
100 g (3½ oz) lightly toasted walnuts
walnut oil, for drizzling
24 slices wagyu bresaola (see note), sliced very thinly (ask your butcher to do this)

dressing

2 tablespoons crème fraîche
2 tablespoons sour cream
2 tablespoons mayonnaise
2 tablespoons plain yoghurt
juice of 1 lemon

SUGAR & SALT-CURED SALMON WITH ASPARAGUS & ORANGE SALAD & GOAT'S CURD

serves 4

method
Mix the rock salt and sugar in a bowl.

Skin the salmon, removing any brown skin on the sides, as well as any bones. Place the salmon on a flat tray, pour the cognac over and rub it into the flesh. Rub both sides of the salmon with the salt and sugar mix. Cover with plastic wrap and leave in the refrigerator for 2 hours to cure.

Rinse the salmon with water, then pat dry with paper towels. Place the salmon on a clean tray and drizzle with a little olive oil. Scatter the dill over the fish and press it on with your fingers. Very thinly slice the salmon using a sharp knife and set aside.

for the asparagus and orange salad
Remove the skins from the oranges using a sharp knife, also discarding the bitter white piths. Cut the oranges into segments, releasing them from their membranes, and removing the seeds as you go.

For the dressing, squeeze any orange juice from the discarded piths and skin into a bowl, then whisk in the olive oil. If you don't have enough juice, take one of the orange segments and squeeze the juice in. Season with sea salt and freshly ground black pepper and set aside.

Half-fill a saucepan with water and add a little sea salt. Bring to a simmer, add the asparagus and blanch for 2 minutes. Remove and cool in an iced-water bath, then drain on paper towels and pat dry.

Add the asparagus to the orange segments, along with the hazelnuts and herbs. Add most of the orange dressing and toss well to combine.

to serve
Lay the salmon slices on four serving plates. Add three dollops of the goat's curd to each plate.

Arrange the salad over the top, drizzle with the remaining orange dressing and serve.

ingredients
160 g (5½ oz/½ cup) rock salt
100 g (3½ oz/½ cup) soft brown sugar
400 g (14 oz) piece of fresh salmon
50 ml (1¾ fl oz) cognac
extra virgin olive oil, for drizzling
½ cup dill, finely chopped
4 tablespoons goat's curd

asparagus & orange salad
2 oranges
100 ml (3½ fl oz) extra virgin olive oil
16 asparagus spears, woody ends
    trimmed
50 g (1¾ oz/⅓ cup) roasted hazelnuts,
    peeled and roughly chopped
½ cup parsley leaves, picked and
    washed
4 tablespoons tarragon leaves,
    picked and washed
250 g (9 oz) punnet baby chard
    or baby beetroot (beet) leaves

PORK & FENNEL SAUSAGE ROLLS WITH GREEN TOMATO CHUTNEY

makes 10–12

ingredients

825 g (1 lb 13 oz) packet ready-made
    puff pastry sheets
2 free-range eggs, beaten

filling

1 tablespoon extra virgin olive oil
1 onion, finely chopped
4 garlic cloves, finely chopped
1 carrot, finely diced
1 celery stalk, finely diced
250 g (9 oz) minced (ground) veal
250 g (9 oz) minced (ground) pork
    shoulder
200 g (7 oz) pork back fat, minced
    (ground)
1 teaspoon chilli flakes
50 ml (1¾ fl oz) cognac
1 tablespoon toasted fennel seeds,
    plus extra fennel seeds for sprinkling
2 free-range eggs
75 g (2½ oz/1¼ cups) fresh breadcrumbs

green tomato chutney

½ teaspoon green cardamom pods
⅛ teaspoon ground turmeric
½ cinnamon stick
1 small garlic clove, finely chopped
1.5 cm (⅝ inch) knob of fresh ginger,
    peeled and finely chopped
½ onion, finely chopped
500 g (1 lb 2 oz) green tomatoes,
    cores removed, finely chopped
½ green apple, peeled, cored and
    chopped
100 g (3½ oz/½ cup) soft brown sugar
45 g (1½ oz/¼ cup) raisins
100 ml (3½ fl oz) cider vinegar

for the green tomato chutney

Crush the cardamom seeds, discarding the pods. Add the cardamom seeds to a large saucepan and toast for 30 seconds over medium heat. Stir in the remaining chutney ingredients and cook for 45 minutes, or until the chutney is nice and thick. Season with sea salt and freshly ground black pepper.

Remove from the heat and spread the chutney on a flat tray, then place in the refrigerator to chill quickly. Once chilled, spoon into sterilised jars and use as required. The chutney will keep in the fridge for 3–4 weeks.

for the filling

Heat the olive oil in a frying pan over medium–high heat. Add the onion and garlic and cook for 3 minutes, without colouring, until tender.

Add the carrot and celery and cook for a further 12–15 minutes, again without colouring, until very soft.

Remove from the heat, then spread on a tray and place in the refrigerator to cool quickly.

Place the veal, pork shoulder and pork back fat in a large mixing bowl. Add the remaining filling ingredients. Mix together well, adding a good amount of seasoning.

Mix the cooled vegetable mixture through, then weigh the filling out in 80 g (2¾ oz) portions.

for the sausage rolls

Cut the puff pastry sheets into 15 x 10 cm (6 x 4 inch) rectangles and place them on a floured work surface.

Place the filling lengthways down the centre of each pastry rectangle, then roll the pastry rectangles into cylinder shapes. Brush a little beaten egg along one side, then seal the pastry together. Rest the sausage rolls in the refrigerator for about 1 hour.

Preheat the oven to 200°C (400°F/Gas 6).

Place the rolls on a baking tray, brush with the remaining egg wash and sprinkle with extra fennel seeds. Bake for 25–30 minutes, or until the pastry is puffed and golden.

Serve warm, with the green tomato chutney.

SEARED WAGYU BEEF CARPACCIO SALAD WITH NAM JIM

serves 6

ingredients

480 g (1 lb 1 oz) piece of wagyu beef or grain-fed beef fillet

salad

30 mint leaves, torn
30 coriander (cilantro) leaves, torn
30 Vietnamese mint leaves, torn
45 g (1½ oz/½ cup) Crisp Shallots (see recipe on page 206)
2 tablespoons toasted sesame seeds (see Crab Omelette recipe on page 46)
1 Lebanese (short) cucumber, peeled and sliced
125 g (4½ oz) heirloom cherry tomatoes, halved

nam jim dressing

5 mild red chillies
5 mild green chillies
1 garlic clove
1 small knob of fresh ginger, peeled
5 coriander (cilantro) roots and stems
100 g (3½ oz/¾ cup) grated palm sugar (jaggery)
60 ml (2 fl oz/¼ cup) fish sauce
juice of 2–3 limes

for the dressing

Roughly chop the chillies, garlic, ginger and coriander roots and stems.

Using a mortar and pestle or blender, pound or crush the mixture until you have a rough paste. Alternatively, chop the ingredients as finely as possible.

Add the palm sugar in small amounts until dissolved. Add the fish sauce and lime juice to taste. Set aside.

for the beef

Heat a barbecue or chargrill pan to medium-high. Season the beef with sea salt and freshly ground black pepper, then sear each side for 2–3 minutes — the beef should still be rare.

Rest the beef on a tray for 5 minutes.

for the salad

While the beef is resting, place the torn herbs in a bowl, along with the shallots, sesame seeds, cucumber and cherry tomatoes. Toss with half the nam jim dressing and season to taste.

to serve

Using a sharp knife, very thinly slice the beef. Season each piece and arrange on a platter or six serving plates.

Scatter the salad over, drizzle with the remaining dressing and serve.

FIG, RED ONION JAM & ROQUEFORT TARTS

serves 4

for the red onion jam

Heat the olive oil in a saucepan over medium–high heat. Add the onion and sauté for 5 minutes, or until softened. Stir in the wine, port, sugar and vinegar and cook until there is no liquid left and the mixture has a jam-like consistency. Season with sea salt and freshly ground black pepper.

Spread the jam onto a clean tray, place a piece of baking paper over the jam and place in the refrigerator to cool completely.

for the tarts

Preheat the oven to 180°C (350°F/Gas 4).

Place the tart shells on a baking tray lined with baking paper. Spread 1½ tablespoons of the red onion jam into each tart.

Roll the four cheese portions into balls and place in the middle of each tart.

Slice each fig into at least eight slices, then wrap these around the balls to ensure the cheese is encased with figs. Drizzle with olive oil and season to taste.

Bake for 10–12 minutes, or until the cheese has softened.

to serve

Place the tarts on four serving plates. Drizzle with the truffle verjuice dressing, garnish with the basil and serve.

ingredients

four 10 cm (4 inch) blind-baked Tart Shells (see recipe on page 206)
½ cup Red Onion Jam (see below)
4 x 35 g (1¼ oz) portions of Roquefort cheese
8 fresh figs
extra virgin olive oil, for drizzling
80 ml (2½ fl oz/⅓ cup) Truffle Verjuice Dressing (see recipe on page 202)
4 tablespoons baby basil leaves

red onion jam

50 ml (1¾ fl oz) extra virgin olive oil
300 g (10½ oz) red onions, sliced
1 litre (35 fl oz/4 cups) red wine
250 ml (9 fl oz/1 cup) port
55 g (2 oz/¼ cup) caster (superfine) sugar
1 tablespoon balsamic vinegar

PORK BELLY WITH STAR ANISE, CAULIFLOWER PURÉE & GREEN MANGO

method

Toast the star anise in a dry frying pan for 20 seconds, then tip onto a small plate. Reserve four of the star anise. Grind the remaining 12 star anise to a powder using a mortar and pestle or a spice grinder, then mix in the salt.

Rub three-quarters of the salt rub over the pork belly, reserving the remaining salt rub. Refrigerate the pork for 1½ hours for the flavours to absorb.

Wash the pork and pat dry with paper towels. Place in a saucepan and cover with the stock. Lightly bash the remaining star anise and add to the pan. Bring to a gentle simmer, then braise the pork for 1½–2 hours. Set aside to cool.

Remove the pork from the braising liquid, reserving the liquid for later use. Cool the pork in the fridge, with a heavy weight on top. (This step can be done 24–48 hours ahead.)

for the green mango

Put the sugar, vinegar and 100 ml (3½ fl oz) water in a saucepan and bring to the boil. Add the coriander roots, ginger and Vietnamese mint stalks. Remove from the heat and allow to infuse for 15 minutes.

Peel the mango using a mandoline or a sharp knife, then julienne long strips of the mango and place in a clean container. Pour the cooled infused liquid over the mango, then cover and marinate in the refrigerator for 24 hours.

Trim the pork neatly and cut into four even pieces.

Heat a small frying pan over medium–high heat. Add the vegetable oil, and bring to the smoking stage.

Season the braised pork belly with the reserved salt rub mixture. Sear the pork pieces in the hot pan for 2 minutes on each side, or until golden brown.

Place the pork in a saucepan and pour the reserved braising liquid over. Cover and heat over medium–low heat until the pork is warm to hot.

to serve

Strain the green mango, then gently toss in a bowl with the coriander and Vietnamese mint leaves.

Spoon the cauliflower purée onto four serving plates, lay a piece of pork alongside and spoon some braising liquid over. Add a mound of green mango salad and serve.

ingredients

16 whole star anise
3½ tablespoons pink salt
500 g (1 lb 2 oz) skinless pork belly
1.5 litres (52 fl oz/6 cups) Pork Stock (see recipe on page 197)
2 tablespoons vegetable oil
20 coriander (cilantro) leaves
20 Vietnamese mint leaves
Cauliflower Purée (see recipe on page 184), to serve

green mango

100 g (3½ oz) sugar
50 ml (1¾ fl oz) white wine vinegar
5 coriander (cilantro) roots, with half the stem
10 g (¼ oz) knob of fresh ginger, peeled and sliced
5 Vietnamese mint stalks, with leaves
1 green mango

LOBSTER SASHIMI WITH WHITE PONZU DRESSING, APPLE & AVOCADO

serves 6

ingredients

1 avocado
½ leek, white part only, julienned
2 live lobsters
1 green apple, julienned
extra virgin olive oil, for drizzling
6 teaspoons fresh wasabi or
    wasabi paste
baby coriander (cilantro) sprigs,
    to garnish

white ponzu dressing

125 ml (4 fl oz/½ cup) white soy sauce
    (see note)
25 ml (¾ fl oz) sesame oil
45 ml (1½ fl oz) rice wine vinegar
1½ tablespoons mirin
1 tablespoon Sugar Syrup
    (see recipe on page 204)
½ piece of kombu seaweed
20 g (¾ oz) fresh ginger, peeled
    and sliced
125 ml (4 fl oz/½ cup) lime juice

for the white ponzu dressing

Place all the dressing ingredients, except the lime juice, in a saucepan. Gently heat until warm.

Remove from the heat and leave to cool slightly, then stir in the lime juice. Cover with plastic wrap and allow to cool naturally. When ready to serve, strain the dressing through a fine sieve.

Cut the avocado in half, then remove the stone and skin. Cover with plastic wrap and place in the freezer.

Half-fill a small saucepan with water, adding a good pinch of sea salt. Bring to the boil, drop in the leek and blanch for 3 minutes. Remove the leek with a slotted spoon and place in an iced-water bath.

When the leek has cooled, place on paper towels and drain off the excess water. Place in a bowl and season with sea salt and freshly ground black pepper.

Place the lobsters in the freezer so that they fall asleep. After about 2 hours, place the lobsters in a large saucepan of salted boiling water and cook for about 3 minutes. Remove them to an iced-water bath to seal the outside and keep the inside quite raw.

When cooled, take the lobsters out of the water and remove the heads using a large sharp knife or kitchen scissors. Using scissors, cut down both sides of the lobster bodies to remove the shell.

Devein the lobsters using a toothpick.

to serve

Place the lobster meat on a chopping board and, using a very sharp knife, thinly slice the flesh. Arrange on a platter or six serving plates and season to taste.

Add the leek and drizzle with the white ponzu dressing. Scatter the apple over.

Remove the avocado from the freezer and grate it over the lobster. Drizzle with olive oil, add a small dollop of wasabi, garnish with baby coriander and serve.

note: White soy sauce, or shiro, has a golden colour and a more subtle, slightly sweeter flavour than regular soy. It is traditionally used for sashimi and is sold in Asian grocers.

CURRIED PARSNIP SOUP

method

Heat the olive oil and butter in a large saucepan. Add the shallot and cook over medium heat without colouring for 5 minutes, or until soft. Add the parsnip and curry powder and cook, stirring, for a further 5 minutes.

Add the milk and cream and bring almost to the boil. Reduce the heat and gently simmer, uncovered, for 30 minutes, being careful not to let the liquid come to the boil.

Allow to cool slightly, then roughly purée using a hand-held blender, or in batches in a food processor or blender.

Gently reheat the soup. Season with sea salt and freshly ground black pepper. Serve garnished with the coriander.

ingredients

60 ml (2 fl oz/¼ cup) extra virgin olive oil

2 tablespoons butter

8 French shallots, thinly sliced

4 large parsnips, peeled and roughly chopped

2 tablespoons good-quality curry powder

1.125 litres (39 fl oz/4½ cups) milk

310 ml (10¾ fl oz/1¼ cups) thin (pouring) cream

2 tablespoons coriander (cilantro) leaves

THAI-STYLE PUMPKIN & COCONUT CREAM SOUP

serves 6

method

Heat the olive oil in a large heavy saucepan over medium heat. Add the shallot, ginger, lemongrass and chilli powder and sauté without browning for 4–5 minutes, or until tender.

Add the pumpkin and stock and bring to the boil. Reduce the heat and gently simmer for 15 minutes, or until the pumpkin is very tender.

Allow the mixture to cool slightly, then transfer to a blender in small amounts and blend to a purée.

Rinse out the saucepan, then pour the pumpkin purée back into it. Stir in the coconut cream and fish sauce, salt and white pepper. Gently heat the soup through, without allowing it to boil. Taste and adjust the seasoning, then stir in the lime juice.

Ladle the soup into six bowls. Garnish with the macadamias and lime leaves and serve.

ingredients

2 tablespoons olive oil

4 French shallots, thinly sliced

60 g (2¼ oz) knob of fresh ginger, peeled and grated

1 tablespoon chopped lemongrass, pale part only

a good pinch of chilli powder

1 kg (2 lb 4 oz) butternut pumpkin (squash), peeled and diced

500 ml (17 fl oz/2 cups) vegetable stock or water

440 ml (15¼ fl oz) can coconut cream

a splash of fish sauce

1½ teaspoons sea salt

½ teaspoon ground white pepper

juice of 1 lime

roasted chopped macadamia nuts, to garnish

2 kaffir lime leaves, finely shredded, to garnish

SMOKED HAM HOCK & VEGETABLE SOUP

serves 6–8

ingredients

2 smoked ham hocks
1.5 litres (52 fl oz/6 cups) Chicken
   Stock (see recipe on page 192)
   or vegetable stock
200 g (7 oz) Jerusalem artichokes
200 g (7 oz) celeriac root
200 g (7 oz) pumpkin (winter squash)
80 ml (2½ fl oz/⅓ cup) extra virgin
   olive oil
1 onion, very finely diced
6 garlic cloves, very finely chopped
¼ savoy cabbage, roughly chopped
200 g (7 oz) frozen or fresh peas
2 zucchini (courgettes), diced
3 tablespoons fresh tarragon leaves

method

Place the ham hocks in a large saucepan and cover with the stock. Bring to a simmer and cook, uncovered, for 1½–2 hours, or until the meat is tender and almost falling off the bone.

Remove the ham hocks from the stock and place them on a tray, allowing them to cool slightly. Strain the stock and set aside.

When the hocks are cool enough to handle, pick the meat off the bones. Discard the bones and any fat, reserving the meat.

Peel the Jerusalem artichokes, celeriac and pumpkin. Cut them into 1 cm (½ inch) dice and set aside.

Heat the olive oil in a large saucepan over medium heat. Add the onion and garlic and cook, without colouring, for 10 minutes, or until both are very tender.

Add the artichokes, celeriac and pumpkin and cook, stirring, for a further 5 minutes.

Add the reserved ham hock stock and bring to the boil, then turn the heat down to a gentle simmer. Now add the ham hock meat, cabbage, peas and zucchini. Simmer for a further 5 minutes, or until the peas are tender, then season to taste with sea salt and freshly ground black pepper.

Just before serving, stir in the tarragon.

Serve the soup with a rustic baguette, spread with good-quality butter.

CRAB & CHARGRILLED CORN SOUP

serves 6

ingredients

2 corn cobs
1 teaspoon sea salt
ground white pepper, for seasoning
extra virgin olive oil, for drizzling
50 g (1¾ oz) unsalted butter
juice of ½ lemon
400 g (14 oz) picked crabmeat
2 kaffir lime leaves, finely shredded
baby coriander (cilantro) leaves,
    to garnish

crab broth

1 kg (2 lb 4 oz) crabs, cleaned
    and washed
100 ml (3½ fl oz) extra virgin olive oil
5 French shallots, sliced
4 garlic cloves, chopped
80 ml (2½ fl oz/⅓ cup) Noilly Prat
    or vermouth
150 ml (5 fl oz) white wine
1 litre (35 fl oz/4 cups) hot Fish Stock
    (see recipe on page 196)
500 ml (17 fl oz/2 cups) thin (pouring)
    cream, heated

for the crab broth

Smash the crabs with a rolling pin to break all the shells.

Heat the olive oil in a large saucepan over medium heat. Add the shallot and garlic and sweat down for 3 minutes, without browning.

Increase the heat to high, add the smashed crabs and cook for 5 minutes, or until they have changed colour.

Deglaze the pan with the vermouth, stirring to dissolve any stuck-on bits, then add the wine and cook for 10 minutes, or until the liquid has reduced by two-thirds.

Pour in the hot stock and bring to the boil. Add the hot cream and return to the boil, then reduce the heat and simmer for 2–3 minutes.

Remove from the heat and allow to cool slightly.

Blend the mixture, including the shells, in three batches in a food processor, passing each batch through a fine sieve, and then through cheesecloth (muslin).

Transfer to a clean saucepan, ready to finish the soup off.

Cook the corn in a saucepan of salted simmering water for 5–7 minutes. Remove with tongs and drain. Season with the salt and white pepper and drizzle with olive oil.

Now cook the corn on a hot barbecue or chargrill pan until nicely charred all over. Remove from the heat and allow to cool slightly, then cut off the corn kernels using a sharp knife. Set aside and keep warm.

to serve

Bring the soup back to the boil. Stir in the butter and lemon juice and season to taste. Blend for 30 seconds using a hand-held blender.

Divide the warm corn and the crabmeat among six serving bowls. Add the lime leaves, then ladle in the soup.

Garnish with baby coriander leaves and serve.

COCONUT BROTH

serves 6

for the broth

Melt the butter in a large saucepan over low heat. Add the shallot, fish and lime leaves and cook for 5 minutes, or until soft.

Add the stock, coconut cream and milk powder and simmer for a further 10 minutes. Remove from the heat and leave the broth to infuse for 20 minutes.

Discard the lime leaves, then blend the broth in a food processor. Strain through a fine sieve and set aside.

To serve, pour back into a clean saucepan and gently reheat, checking the seasoning.

for the garnish

Melt the palm sugar in a small saucepan with 150 ml (5 fl oz) water. Add the lime zest and lime leaf and cook for 2 minutes. Set aside.

(The garnish can be made 24 hours in advance and stored in a clean airtight container in the fridge.)

to serve

Sprinkle a little spice mix into six soup bowls or soup terrines, then ladle the broth over the top.

Serve topped with the garnish, coriander and nori.

note: Luke Mangan's Sydney Spice is a tangy, zesty spice blend available from www.lukemangan.com and selected fine food stores.

broth

50 g (1¾ oz) butter
100 g (3½ oz) French shallots, very finely diced
50 g (1¾ oz) white fish flesh (preferably not from a strong oily fish)
6 kaffir lime leaves
400 ml (14 fl oz) Fish Stock (see recipe on page 196)
400 ml (14 fl oz) coconut cream
100 g (3½ oz) coconut milk powder

garnish

50 g (1¾ oz) palm sugar (jaggery)
zest of ½ lime
1 kaffir lime leaf, finely shredded

to serve

3 tablespoons Luke Mangan's Sydney Spice (see note)
½ cup finely chopped baby coriander (cilantro) leaves
1 sheet nori (dried seaweed), finely shredded

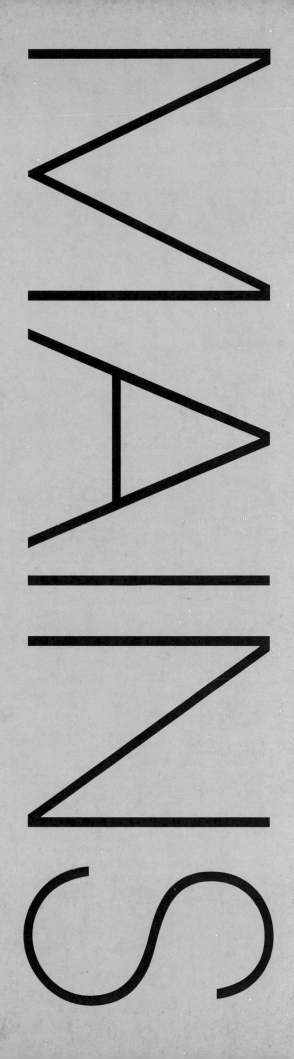

MAINS

Many of the mains in this chapter are signature dishes straight from my Salt grill restaurants — light and approachable, without following food trends.

I love cooking outdoors when I'm at home, so I've also included some meat dishes that can be done on a barbecue and served with a variety of sides. For instance, I really love the Barbecued T-bone recipe (page 109) with my mum's Zucchini Slice (page 186).

Keeping with the theme of this book, I've also included a variety of mains that are suitable for sharing — such as the Baked Flathead with Prosciutto, Tomato & Parsley (page 91), which looks fabulous in the middle of the table.

For me, sharing food at a table with friends is one of life's greatest joys!

WHOLE BABY BARRAMUNDI WITH ASIAN VEGETABLES & CRABMEAT

serves 4 as a shared dish

ingredients

1.6 kg (3 lb 8 oz) whole baby
    barramundi, scaled and washed
½ cup coriander (cilantro) leaves,
    to garnish (reserve the stalks for
    the vegetables below)
lime cheeks, to serve

vegetables

80 ml (2½ fl oz/⅓ cup) extra virgin
    olive oil, plus extra for drizzling
3 French shallots, thinly sliced
3 garlic cloves, thinly sliced
2 mild chillies, sliced
reserved coriander (cilantro) stalks
    (from above), finely chopped
100 g (3½ oz) fresh shiitake
    mushrooms, stalks removed, sliced
100 g (3½ oz) oyster mushrooms, torn
6 kaffir lime leaves, stalks removed
    and thinly sliced
100 ml (3½ fl oz) oyster sauce
50 ml (1¾ fl oz) hoisin sauce
2 bok choy (pak choy), washed
    and cut into quarters
3 choy sum, washed and sliced
    on an angle
200 g (7 oz) cooked blue swimmer
    crabmeat

for the vegetables

Heat a large frying pan over medium–high heat. Add the olive oil and begin sweating off the shallot, garlic, chilli and coriander stalks for 2 minutes without browning.

Add the mushrooms and lime leaves and cook for a further 3–4 minutes, or until the mushrooms are cooked. Add the oyster sauce, hoisin sauce and 200 ml (7 fl oz) water and bring to the boil. Remove from the heat and transfer to a bowl.

Add the bok choy and choy sum to a saucepan of simmering water and cook for 1 minute, then drain and place in iced water.

Drain the cooled greens on paper towels, then roughly chop and add to the mushroom mixture, along with the crabmeat. Season with sea salt and freshly ground black pepper and toss together.

Preheat the oven to 180°C (350°F/Gas 4).

Place the fish on a chopping board. From the belly side, run a sharp knife down each side of the backbone to open up the fish.

Using kitchen scissors, cut the bone at the top near the head, and the bone near the tail, to remove the centre bone and completely open the fish.

Place the fish on a large tray lined with baking paper. Place the bok choy and mushroom mixture inside the fish, adding the sauce from the vegetables, and fold over the flap so that it resembles a whole fish again.

Bake the fish for 35–40 minutes. To check if the fish is ready, insert a knife in the middle to see if the flesh is white; if it isn't, cook for a further 5–10 minutes.

When the fish is done, remove from the oven and rest for 5 minutes before transferring to a large serving platter.

Lightly season the fish. Drizzle with the juice from the baking tray and a little olive oil. Garnish with the coriander and serve with lime cheeks.

WHOLE CORN-FED CHICKEN POACHED WITH ROOT VEGETABLES & SERVED WITH GREEN SAUCE

serves 4–6

for the green sauce

Place all the ingredients in a blender and blend well until you have a smooth green paste. Transfer to a clean container and store in the refrigerator.

(This sauce can be made 1 day ahead. Keep in the fridge and bring back to room temperature before serving.)

Wash the chicken in cold water and place in a stockpot. Pour in the stock and add the ginger and bouquet garni.

Add the bacon, salt and garlic and bring to the boil. Reduce the heat to a simmer, then add the swede and potato and cook for about 10 minutes.

Now add the carrots, onions, fennel, cabbage and turnips and cook for 5 minutes, then add the broad beans.

Carefully remove the chicken from the pot and allow to rest for 5 minutes in a deep dish.

Discard the bouquet garni and transfer the vegetables and chicken to a serving platter.

Season the liquid in the pot with sea salt and freshly ground black pepper, then pour a little over the chicken and the vegetables.

Serve hot, with the green sauce on the side.

note: To make a bouquet garni, place 10 thyme sprigs, 2 teaspoons black peppercorns, 20 marjoram sprigs and 4 fresh bay leaves on a piece of muslin (cheesecloth). Tie the ends of the cloth together, to make a small herb parcel.

ingredients

1.8 kg (4 lb) corn-fed, free-range, organic chicken
2.5 litres (87 fl oz/10 cups) Chicken Stock (see recipe on page 192) or water
80 g (2¾ oz) fresh ginger, peeled and sliced
1 bouquet garni (see note)
500 g (1 lb 2 oz) unsliced bacon
½ teaspoon fine sea salt
14 garlic cloves, lightly bashed
1 large swede (rutabaga), peeled and cut into chunks
4 kipfler (fingerling) potatoes, cut in half
8 baby heirloom carrots, washed
8 baby onions, tops cleaned
2 small fennel bulbs, cut in half
¼ savoy cabbage, cut into chunks
8 baby turnips
400 g (14 oz) fresh broad beans, blanched and peeled

green sauce

25 sultanas (golden raisins), soaked in port for at least 30 minutes
375 ml (13 fl oz/1½ cups) extra virgin olive oil
2 garlic cloves
1 bird's eye chilli, chopped
3 anchovies
2 tablespoons dijon mustard
1½ tablespoons capers
150 g (5½ oz) flat-leaf (Italian) parsley
150 g (5½ oz) mint leaves
150 g (5½ oz) basil leaves
juice of ½ lemon
1 tablespoon cabernet sauvignon vinegar or red wine vinegar
75 ml (2¼ fl oz) warm water

BARBECUED DRY-AGED RIB EYE WITH BRUSSELS SPROUTS, BACON & ROSEMARY

serves 2–4 as a shared dish

ingredients

1 kg (2 lb 4 oz) piece of dry-aged rib eye

2 tablespoons ras el hanout (see notes)

extra virgin olive oil, for drizzling

1 tablespoon freshly ground black pepper

1 tablespoon pink salt or sea salt

Brussels Sprouts with Bacon and Rosemary (see recipe on page 177), to serve

method

Put the beef on a tray. Rub the ras el hanout and a little olive oil all over the beef, coating it evenly. Wrap in plastic wrap and refrigerate for at least 12 hours, or overnight if time permits.

The next day, remove the beef from the fridge and allow the meat to come to room temperature — this will take about 45 minutes.

Heat a barbecue grill to medium–high. Season the beef with the pepper and pink salt. Place the beef on the grill, then cook with the lid down for 15–18 minutes on each side.

Remove from the grill and rest the beef in a warm place for 8 minutes.

Slice the beef on the diagonal and arrange on a serving platter. Drizzle with a little more olive oil and season to taste.

Serve with a side dish of brussels sprouts with bacon and rosemary.

notes: Ras el hanout is a heady north African spice blend, containing dozens of different aromatics such as cumin, cinnamon, cardamom, ginger, anise, nutmeg, peppercorn, clove, chilli, coriander, turmeric and even dried flowers. You'll find it in spice shops and fine food stores.

For this recipe you'll need a barbecue with a hood or lid.

RAINBOW TROUT WITH FREGOLA, CUCUMBER & TOMATO BROTH

method

Place the fregola in a saucepan with half the stock. Season with sea salt and freshly ground black pepper and bring to the boil. Reduce the heat to a simmer and cook for 20 minutes, or until just tender. Drain and set aside.

Preheat the oven to 180°C (350°F/Gas 4).

Season the flesh side of the trout fillets. Heat the olive oil in a frying pan and add the fish, skin side down. Cook over medium–high heat for 1 minute on each side.

Transfer the fish to a baking tray and bake for 1–2 minutes. Remove from the oven and leave to rest for 2 minutes.

Pour the remaining stock into a saucepan and bring to the boil. Add the fregola, cucumber, tomatoes and butter and season to taste. Bring to a good simmer, stirring the ingredients together. Remove from the heat, then stir in the lemon juice and dill.

To serve, ladle the fregola mixture into four serving bowls and place the fish on top. Drizzle with a little more olive oil and serve.

note: Fregola is a Sicilian pasta made from semolina, similar in appearance to large balls of couscous. After being rolled into balls, the pasta is toasted, giving a slightly nutty texture.

ingredients

100 g (3½ oz) fregola (see note)

400 ml (14 fl oz) Fish Stock (see recipe on page 196)

4 x 200 g (7 oz) rainbow trout fillets, skin on

2 tablespoons extra virgin olive oil, plus extra for drizzling

4 vine-ripened tomatoes, cut into 2 cm (¾ inch) dice

1 telegraph (long) cucumber, cut into 2 cm (¾ inch) dice

75 g (2½ oz) butter

juice of 3 lemons

3 tablespoons finely chopped dill

ROASTED BARRAMUNDI WITH PRESERVED LEMON & BASIL RISOTTO & SWEET PEA SAUCE

serves 6

ingredients

60 ml (2 fl oz/¼ cup) extra virgin
    olive oil
6 x 150 g (5½ oz) barramundi fillets,
    skin on
basil leaves, to garnish

risotto

50 ml (1¾ fl oz) extra virgin olive oil
100 g (3½ oz) unsalted butter
1 onion, finely chopped
500 g (1 lb 2 oz/2¼ cups) arborio rice
100 ml (3½ fl oz) white wine
2 litres (70 fl oz/8 cups) hot Fish Stock
    (see recipe on page 196)
1 tablespoon chopped lemon thyme
1 cup chopped basil
½ cup chopped flat-leaf (Italian)
    parsley
1 tablespoon chopped chervil
1½ tablespoons preserved lemon rind,
    finely chopped (see notes on
    page 93)
150 g (5½ oz/1½ cups) finely grated
    good-quality parmesan cheese

sweet pea sauce

20 g (¾ oz) butter
1 small onion, sliced
50 ml (1¾ fl oz) white wine
600 ml (21 fl oz) hot Fish Stock
    (see recipe on page 196)
500 g (1 lb 2 oz) frozen peas, thawed

to make the risotto

Heat the olive oil and 30 g (1 oz) of the butter in a large heavy-based saucepan. Add the onion and fry gently for 5–7 minutes, until softened but not browned.

Add the rice and stir constantly until the grains are hot.

Pour in the wine and continue to cook until the liquid has almost evaporated. Reduce the heat and gradually add the hot stock, a ladleful at a time, stirring the rice constantly. As the rice absorbs the liquid, continue to add more hot stock until the rice is cooked — this will take about 30 minutes.

Stir in the chopped herbs, preserved lemon rind and remaining butter. Fold the parmesan through, then check the seasoning and add more to taste, if needed.

to make the sweet pea sauce

Melt the butter in a medium saucepan, add the onion and gently cook for 4–5 minutes, or until softened.

Add the wine, bring to the boil and cook until the liquid has reduced by half.

Add the hot stock and return to the boil, then add the peas and cook for 3 minutes. Season with sea salt and freshly ground black pepper.

Strain the peas, reserving the liquid. Purée the peas in a blender, adding enough of the reserved liquid to achieve a soup consistency. Set aside.

Meanwhile, preheat the oven to 180°C (350°F/Gas 4).

Heat the extra virgin olive oil in a large frying pan. Add the fish fillets, skin side down, and cook over medium–high heat until lightly browned on both sides.

Place the fillets on a baking tray, transfer to the oven and bake for 5–7 minutes, or until just cooked through.

to serve

Pour the sweet pea sauce onto six serving plates. Spoon the risotto onto one side of the plate and place a barramundi fillet alongside, skin side up. Garnish with a few basil leaves and serve.

BAKED FLATHEAD WITH PROSCIUTTO, TOMATO & PARSLEY

serves 4

method

Preheat the oven to 180°C (350°F/Gas 4).

Grease a baking dish with the butter.

Lay the onion slices evenly over the base of the dish, then layer the potato slices over the onion. Lightly season with sea salt and freshly ground black pepper.

Pour the stock over and bake for 25 minutes, or until the potato is tender.

Meanwhile, neatly trim the flathead fillets and remove as many bones as you can.

Remove the baking dish from the oven and drape the prosciutto over the potato. Lay the fish fillets on top.

Return to the oven and bake for a further 6–8 minutes, or until the fish is just cooked through.

Sprinkle the chopped tomato and parsley over.

Serve from the baking dish at the table.

ingredients

50 g (1¾ oz) butter, for greasing

2 large onions, thinly sliced

4 large potatoes, peeled and thinly sliced

1 litre (35 fl oz/4 cups) Fish Stock (see recipe on page 196)

8 flathead fillets, or 4 halved fillets if large, skin on

8 slices prosciutto

3 vine-ripened tomatoes, chopped

1 cup flat-leaf (Italian) parsley leaves, roughly chopped

ROASTED PORK BELLY WITH ROASTED PEARS & SWEDE MASH

serves 4–6

ingredients
1.5 kg (3 lb 5 oz) pork belly
Swede Mash (see recipe on
    page 178), to serve

roasted pears
3 corella or bosc pears, quartered
    but not cored
50 g (1¾ oz) sugar
100 g (3½ oz) unsalted butter
a splash of Poire Williams or pear liqueur
150 ml (5 fl oz) Pork Stock (see recipe
    on page 197)

method
Preheat the oven to 220°C (425°F/Gas 7).

Place the pork belly on a clean work surface, skin side up. With a small sharp knife, score the pork in a diamond or crisscross pattern, about 5 mm (¼ inch) apart, through the skin and into the fat, ensuring you don't cut into the meat.

Rub sea salt into all the scores, pulling the skin apart a little if you need to. Brush any excess salt off the skin, then turn the pork over. Season the underside of the meat with a little more sea salt and a little freshly ground black pepper.

Place the pork, skin side up, in a large roasting tin and transfer to the oven. Roast for about 30 minutes, or until the skin of the pork puffs up and begins to resemble a crackling.

Reduce the oven temperature to 170°C (325°F/Gas 3) and roast for another 1½ hours.

Remove the pork from the oven and baste with the tray juices — the meat should be very soft and tender.

Carefully transfer the pork to a tray, cover with foil and set aside to rest for 10 minutes.

for the roasted pears
Heat a large ovenproof frying pan over medium heat. Add the pears, sugar and butter and cook for 2 minutes, or until the pears have a nice colouring.

Transfer the pan to the oven and roast the pears for about 5 minutes. Place the pan back on the stovetop. Add a good splash of liqueur and allow to reduce by half, then stir in the stock and allow to reduce again for 2–3 minutes.

Take the pan off the heat.

to serve
Slice the pork and place on a serving platter. Arrange the pears on top, pour the liqueur sauce over.

Serve with swede mash on the side.

HERB-CRUSTED SIRLOIN WITH ROASTED SHALLOTS & MADEIRA JUS

serves 4

method

Bring the steaks to room temperature.

Meanwhile, preheat the oven to 160°C (315°F/Gas 2–3).

Heat a large frying pan over medium heat. Add the olive oil and the shallots, skin side down, and cook for 10 minutes, or until golden underneath.

Remove the shallots to a baking tray lined with baking paper and bake for 20–25 minutes, or until tender.

Remove from the oven and allow to cool, then carefully remove the outer skins.

for the herb crust

Combine the mustard, preserved lemon and horseradish in a small bowl. Set aside.

In a blender, pulse the herbs and breadcrumbs until the mixture is completely green in colour, then remove to a bowl and set aside.

Season the steaks with sea salt and freshly ground black pepper. Place on a hot chargrill and cook until desired — 3 minutes on each side for rare; 5 minutes on each side for medium-rare; 10 minutes on each side for well done. Remove from the heat and rest for 5 minutes.

Meanwhile, preheat the oven grill (broiler) to medium. Heat the madeira sauce in a saucepan until warm.

Smear the mustard mixture evenly over the rested steaks, then cover with the herb mix. Place under the grill with the shallots and cook for 2 minutes, or until the crust is golden.

to serve

Slice the steaks, then arrange on four serving plates with the shallots. Serve with the warm madeira jus.

notes: Preserved lemons are sold in jars in delicatessens and selected grocers and feature prominently in north African cuisines. Only the outer rind is used; discard any fleshy pulp as it is salty, tough and bitter.

Panko breadcrumbs are large, crisp, white breadcrumbs used in Japanese dishes such as tempura. You'll find them in good food stores and larger supermarkets.

ingredients

4 x 250 g (9 oz) sirloin portions
60 ml (2 fl oz/¼ cup) extra virgin olive oil
16 French shallots, skin on, cut in half
½ quantity Madeira Sauce (see recipe on page 199)

herb crust

1 tablespoon dijon mustard
1 teaspoon finely diced preserved lemon rind (see notes)
2 teaspoons grated fresh horseradish
1 cup parsley, finely chopped
4 tablespoons tarragon, finely chopped
20 mint leaves, finely chopped
4 tablespoons panko breadcrumbs (see notes)

MOROCCAN SNAPPER & SHELLFISH HOTPOT WITH LIME PICKLE

serves 4

ingredients

4 x 180 g (6 oz) snapper fillets, skin on
16 mussels, scrubbed well, hairy
    beards removed
16 large purged clams (vongole),
    scrubbed
8 large raw prawns (shrimp), peeled
    and deveined, tails left intact
4 cups silverbeet (Swiss chard),
    blanched and chopped
20 black olives, halved and pitted
½ cup roughly chopped coriander
    (cilantro) leaves
3 tablespoons chopped mint leaves
Lime Pickle (see recipe on page 203),
    to serve

chermoula

100 g (3½ oz) coriander (cilantro),
    roughly chopped
5 garlic cloves, chopped
3 teaspoons ground cumin
1½ red finger chillies (see note),
    seeded and roughly chopped
75 ml (2¼ fl oz) extra virgin olive oil
juice of 2 lemons
1 tablespoon sweet paprika
2 teaspoons sea salt

moroccan sauce

2 tablespoons olive oil, plus extra
    for brushing
5 celery stalks, diced
2 carrots, diced
2 small onions, diced
500 g (1 lb 2 oz/2 cups) chopped
    tinned tomatoes
½ teaspoon saffron threads
½ preserved lemon (see notes on
    page 93), rind finely chopped
8 kipfler (fingerling) potatoes, cut
    lengthways into quarters
1.75 litres (61 fl oz/7 cups) Fish Stock
    (see recipe on page 196)

for the chermoula

Place all the ingredients in a food processor and blend to a smooth paste. Transfer to a clean container and set aside.

(The chermoula can be made 1 day ahead. Cover and refrigerate until required.)

for the moroccan sauce

Heat the olive oil in a large saucepan. Add the celery, carrot and onion and fry gently for 10 minutes, until softened but not browned.

Add the tomatoes and saffron and cook until the tomatoes begin to break down.

Stir in half the preserved lemon rind and half the chermoula and sauté for a few minutes, or until fragrant.

Add the potatoes and cook for a further 5 minutes.

Pour in the stock and bring to the boil, then reduce the heat and simmer for 25 minutes.

to serve

Spread the remaining chermoula over the snapper and add to the saucepan with the mussels, clams, prawns and silverbeet.

Bring to a simmer and cook for 8–10 minutes, or until the fish and prawns are just cooked and the clams and mussels have opened, discarding any clams or mussels that haven't opened.

Stir in the olives, coriander, mint and remaining preserved lemon, then season if needed with sea salt and freshly ground black pepper.

Serve with lime pickle on the side.

note: Also called cayenne chillies, red finger chillies are thin, thick-fleshed chillies about 15 cm (6 inches) long. They are very fiery, so handle carefully when seeding and chopping them.

CHICKEN TAGINE WITH BAKED SWEET POTATO

serves 6

method

Preheat the oven to 190°C (375°F/Gas 5).

Place the chicken, baharat, olive oil and honey in a large bowl. Season with sea salt and freshly ground black pepper and mix well, ensuring the chicken is well coated. Set aside.

Heat a little olive oil in a tagine or heavy-based flameproof casserole dish over medium heat. Add the sweet potato, onion and garlic and sauté for 5 minutes.

Add the chicken and cook on all sides until just sealed. Pour in the stock and mix a little to combine. Cover with a tight-fitting lid, transfer to the oven and bake for 30 minutes.

Add the currants and port to the tagine. Bake, uncovered, for a further 15 minutes.

for the fennel pilaff

While the chicken is cooking, place the rice in a rice cooker with the fennel seeds, stock and some seasoning. Cook the rice until all the liquid has been absorbed, or as per your rice cooker instructions.

(If you don't have a rice cooker, heat the stock and fennel seeds in a saucepan, stir in the rice and simmer for 15–20 minutes. Turn off the heat, then cover and allow to stand for about 10 minutes before serving.)

to serve

Garnish the tagine with the pistachios and serve with the pilaff.

note: Baharat is an aromatic spice mix available from spice shops and fine food stores. Although actual blends vary widely throughout the Middle East and northern Africa, baharat (Arabic for 'spice') often contains spices such as ground black peppercorns, cumin, cinnamon, cardamom, coriander seeds, nutmeg, cloves and paprika.

ingredients

1 kg (2 lb 4 oz) free-range boneless, skinless chicken thighs
1 tablespoon baharat (see note)
1½ tablespoons extra virgin olive oil, plus extra for pan-frying
1½ tablespoons honey
2 sweet potatoes, peeled and cut into 2 cm (¾ inch) cubes
1 onion, finely chopped
6 garlic cloves, crushed
250 ml (9 fl oz/1 cup) Chicken Stock (see recipe on page 192)
50 g (1¾ oz/⅓ cup) currants, soaked in port for 1 hour
80 g (2¾ oz) toasted pistachio nuts, chopped, to garnish

fennel pilaff

400 g (14 oz/2 cups) long-grain white rice, rinsed and drained three times
1 teaspoon fennel seeds
700 ml (24 fl oz) Chicken Stock (see recipe on page 192)

FLOUNDER À LA MEUNIÈRE WITH PRAWNS & SPECK

serves 4

ingredients

4 x 450 g (1 lb) whole flounder,
    cleaned and gutted
50 g (1¾ oz/⅓ cup) plain
    (all-purpose) flour
80 ml (2½ fl oz/⅓ cup) extra virgin
    olive oil
425 g (15 oz) unsalted butter
100 g (3½ oz) speck, or good-quality
    unsliced bacon, diced
8 raw prawns (shrimp), peeled and
    deveined, each chopped into
    4 pieces
2 tablespoons salted baby capers,
    soaked in water for 2 hours,
    then drained
4 tablespoons roughly chopped
    parsley
80 ml (2½ fl oz/⅓ cup) lemon juice

method

Preheat the oven to 160°C (315°F/Gas 2–3).

Wash the fish and pat dry with a cloth. Season with sea salt and freshly ground black pepper, then dust each fish with the flour and pat off any excess.

Heat 1 tablespoon of the olive oil and 70 g (2½ oz) of the butter in a non-stick frying pan over medium–high heat.

Add one or two fish, depending on the size of your pan, and cook for 2 minutes, or until golden brown underneath.

Turn the fish over and repeat on the other side. Transfer the fish to a tray lined with baking paper.

Cook the remaining fish in the same way, adding more of the olive oil and butter each time.

Transfer the fish to the oven and bake for about 8 minutes, or until just cooked through.

While the fish is cooking in the oven, wipe the pan clean and place over medium heat.

Add the remaining butter to the pan, along with the speck. When the butter begins to foam and bubble and turn a nutty brown colour, add the prawns and cook for 30 seconds.

Immediately remove from the heat and add the capers, parsley and lemon juice. Season to taste.

to serve

Remove the fish from the oven and place on four serving plates. Pour the butter mixture over the fish and serve.

LOBSTER THERMIDOR

method

Place the lobsters in the freezer so that they fall asleep. After about 2 hours, half-fill a steamer, wok or large saucepan with water and bring to a rapid boil over high heat. Working one at a time if necessary, place the lobsters in the steamer, then cover and steam for 3 minutes. Cool in an ice bath.

Cut the lobsters through the middle with a sharp knife, lengthways.

Remove the tail meat, reserving the shells. Roughly chop the meat and place in a bowl.

Preheat the oven to 180°C (350°F/Gas 4).

Melt the butter in a sauté pan over medium heat. Add the shallot and garlic and sweat down without colouring, for 3–4 minutes, or until tender. Add the flour and stir through, then continue to cook slowly for 2 minutes.

Deglaze the pan with the cognac, stirring to dissolve any cooked-on bits, and cook out the alcohol for about 30 seconds.

Stir in the stock and cream and cook until reduced by half.

Add the mustard, lemon juice, herbs, cayenne pepper and half the parmesan. Season with sea salt and freshly ground black pepper and leave to cool to room temperature.

Stir the egg yolks into the cream sauce, then pour the sauce into the bowl of lobster meat and combine.

Place the lobster meat back in the lobster shells. Sprinkle with the remaining parmesan.

Place the lobsters on a baking tray and into the oven. Bake for about 10 minutes, or until the cheese is golden.

Serve immediately, with the lemon wedges.

ingredients

2 x 1.2 kg (2 lb 10 oz) live lobsters
2 tablespoons unsalted butter
2 French shallots, very finely diced
2 garlic cloves, finely chopped
1 tablespoon plain (all-purpose) flour
200 ml (7 fl oz) cognac
250 ml (9 fl oz/1 cup) Fish Stock
    (see recipe on page 196)
150 ml (5 fl oz) thick (double) cream
1 tablespoon dijon mustard
juice of ½ lemon
6 tablespoons tarragon, chopped
4 tablespoons chervil, chopped
4 tablespoons chives, chopped
a pinch of cayenne pepper
150 g (5½ oz/1½ cups) grated
    parmesan cheese
2 free-range egg yolks
2 lemons, cut into wedges

PORTUGUESE MARYLAND CHICKEN WITH CHORIZO, CORN, BARBECUED CHILLIES & OLIVES

serves 4

for the chicken marinade

Place the chicken marinade ingredients in a large bowl and mix well to combine.

Cut the leg and thigh sections of the chicken in half, to give two separate pieces. Cut the breast pieces in half also.

Add the chicken pieces to the mixing bowl and coat well with the marinade. Add the chillies, piquillo peppers, chorizo and olives and mix through. Cover and marinate in the refrigerator for 24 hours.

The next day, preheat the oven to 180°C (350°F/Gas 4).

Preheat a barbecue or chargrill pan to medium–high.

Add the salt to a saucepan of simmering water, then add the corn cobs and cook for 5–6 minutes. Remove the corn with tongs and place on a tray. Drizzle with olive oil and season with sea salt and freshly ground black pepper.

Remove the mixing bowl from the fridge and separate the chicken pieces, chorizo, chillies and piquillo peppers from the marinade. Keep the marinade and olives aside.

Chargrill the chicken pieces for 5–6 minutes, or until nicely charred. Chargrill the chorizo, chillies and piquillo peppers for 2–3 minutes. Once charred, transfer everything to a roasting tin. Add the olives, pour the marinade over and bake in the oven for 12–15 minutes.

Meanwhile, place the corn on the barbecue and cook for 4–6 minutes, turning every minute or so, until nice and chargrilled. Remove to a serving dish, drizzle with the chipotle mayonnaise and sprinkle with the parmesan.

Transfer the chicken mixture to a serving dish. Check the seasoning and pour the pan juices over. Garnish with coriander and serve.

notes: Piquillo peppers are sweet red roasted Spanish chillies, available in tins from gourmet grocers; strain before using.

Harissa is a fiery Tunisian chilli paste. Look for it in small tins or tubes at good delicatessens.

ingredients

1–1.2 kg (2 lb 4 oz–2 lb 10 oz) corn-fed, free-range, organic chicken, legs and breasts separated (ask your butcher to do this if you prefer)
8 red finger chillies (see note on page 94)
12 tinned piquillo peppers (see notes)
3 cured chorizo sausages, peeled and cut in half
3 tablespoons black olives
3 tablespoons green olives
1 teaspoon sea salt
2 large corn cobs, husks and silks removed, cut in half crossways
extra virgin olive oil, for drizzling
Chipotle Mayonnaise (see Prawn Toasts recipe on page 13)
100 g (3½ oz/1 cup) finely grated parmesan cheese
coriander (cilantro) leaves, to garnish

chicken marinade

2 tablespoons dried oregano
1 teaspoon harissa (see notes)
1½ tablespoons smoked paprika
2 tablespoons sweet paprika
2 teaspoons cumin seeds, toasted and lightly bashed
2 teaspoons coriander seeds, toasted and lightly bashed
5 rosemary sprigs, leaves picked
2 teaspoons freshly ground black peppercorns
3 teaspoons sea salt
2 tablespoons caster (superfine) sugar
2 lemons, cut into quarters
250 ml (9 fl oz/1 cup) extra virgin olive oil

POACHED SALMON WITH CURRIED SPINACH PURÉE, CRAB SALAD & COCONUT BROTH

serves 4

ingredients

750 ml (26 fl oz/3 cups) Fish Stock
    (see recipe on page 196)
250 ml (9 fl oz/1 cup) white wine
1 teaspoon black peppercorns
3 fresh bay leaves
7 thyme sprigs
4 parsley stalks
4 x 180 g (6 oz) salmon fillets, skin and
    bones removed
½ quantity Coconut Broth (see recipe
    on page 79)

curried spinach purée

1 tablespoon extra virgin olive oil
¼ red onion, sliced
2 garlic cloves, sliced
2 tablespoons good curry powder
1 tablespoon ground ginger
2 tablespoons tomato paste
    (concentrated purée)
2 tomatoes, blanched, peeled,
    seeded and diced
200 ml (7 fl oz) hot Fish Stock
    (see recipe on page 196)
200 g (7 oz) English spinach leaves,
    blanched

crab salad

1 baby fennel bulb, shaved
160 g (5½ oz) blue swimmer crabmeat
16 basil leaves
16 coriander (cilantro) leaves
16 mint leaves
juice of 1 lime
2 teaspoons fish sauce
2 tablespoons extra virgin olive oil
3 tablespoons Crisp Shallots
    (see recipe on page 206)

for the curried spinach purée

Heat the olive oil in a frying pan over medium heat. Sauté the onion and garlic for 8–10 minutes, or until they turn a light caramel colour.

Stir in the spices and cook for a few minutes.

Add the tomato paste and allow to cook out for 2 minutes. Stir in the diced tomatoes and cook for 10–15 minutes, or until you have a thick purée.

Stir in the hot stock and bring to the boil, then reduce the heat and simmer for about 15 minutes. Add the spinach and cook for 1 minute.

Transfer the mixture to a blender and blend until you have a nice smooth purée. Transfer to a bowl and place over an ice bath to cool quickly to keep the nice green colour.

for the poached salmon

Place a large saucepan on the stove. Add the stock, wine, peppercorns, bay leaves, thyme and parsley. Season with sea salt and freshly ground black pepper and bring to a simmer.

Add the salmon and cook for 2–3 minutes on each side. Remove the salmon to a tray, season to taste, and allow to rest. Discard the poaching broth.

for the crab salad

Place all the crab salad ingredients in a bowl and lightly mix.

to serve

Warm the curried spinach purée in a saucepan over medium heat. Meanwhile, warm the coconut broth in a separate saucepan, then transfer the coconut broth to a jug for serving at the table.

Place a spoonful of the spinach purée onto four serving plates. Add the fish and top with the crab salad. Serve with the jug of coconut broth.

BRAISED BEEF CHEEKS WITH CHOCOLATE, JALAPEÑO & BAKED CELERIAC

serves 8

method

Place the beef cheeks in a large container.

Roughly chop the onion, ginger, carrot and celery and place in the container, along with the garlic and herbs.

Combine the port and wine in a saucepan and bring to the boil. Turn the heat down and simmer until the liquid has reduced by half. Remove from the heat and allow to cool. When lukewarm, pour the liquid over the beef cheeks and mix together.

Allow the mixture to cool to room temperature, then cover and refrigerate. Leave to marinate for 24 hours.

The next day, preheat the oven to 140°C (275°F/Gas 1).

Strain the beef mixture, reserving the marinade. Set aside the vegetables and herbs.

Heat the olive oil in a large flameproof casserole dish over medium–high heat. Evenly brown the beef, then remove and set aside.

Add the reserved vegetables to the casserole dish and brown them evenly, then add the reserved marinade and bring to the boil. Reduce the heat and simmer until the liquid has reduced by half.

In a separate saucepan, bring the stock to the boil.

Add the beef, reserved herbs, jalapeño and hot stock to the casserole dish and bring to a gentle simmer. Cover with a tight-fitting lid, transfer to the oven and braise for 4 hours, or until the beef is tender.

Remove from the oven and allow to rest for 10 minutes.

Remove the beef with a slotted spoon and place on a tray. Strain the liquid into a clean saucepan and bring back to the boil. Remove from the heat and whisk in the chocolate, to taste.

to serve

Arrange the beef on a platter or eight serving plates and season with sea salt and freshly ground black pepper.

Pour the chocolate sauce over and serve with baked celeriac and roasted carrots.

ingredients

8 x 300 g (10½ oz) beef cheeks
1 onion
50 g (1¾ oz) knob of fresh ginger, peeled
1 carrot
2 celery stalks
7 garlic cloves
10 thyme sprigs
3 fresh bay leaves
150 ml (5 fl oz) port
750 ml (26 fl oz/3 cups) red wine
60 ml (2 fl oz/¼ cup) olive oil
3 litres (105 fl oz/12 cups) Beef Stock (see recipe on page 193)
2 teaspoons flaked dried jalapeño chilli
200 g (7 oz) good-quality dark chocolate (72% cocoa), or to taste
Baked Celeriac (see recipe on page 177), to serve
Roasted Heirloom Carrots with Dukkah (see recipe on page 178), to serve

CRUMBED PORK CUTLETS WITH FIG, ASPARAGUS, PROSCIUTTO & BÉARNAISE SAUCE

serves 6

ingredients

6 pork cutlets, fat trimmed
6 tablespoons extra virgin olive oil,
    plus extra for drizzling
12 tablespoons ghee (clarified butter)
1 teaspoon sea salt
18 asparagus spears, peeled
6 fresh ripe figs, cut in half
12 slices prosciutto
lemon cheeks, to serve
1 quantity warm Béarnaise Sauce
    (see recipe on page 200)

breadcrumb mix

2 free-range eggs
80 ml (2½ fl oz/⅓ cup) milk
150 g (5½ oz) panko breadcrumbs
    (see notes on page 93)
250 g (9 oz) dukkah (see note on
    page 178)
50 g (1¾ oz/⅓ cup) plain
    (all-purpose) flour

method

Preheat the oven to 180°C (350°F/Gas 4).

With the pork cutlets, clean the top of the bones with a sharp knife to ensure there is no meat left on the bone.

Place the cutlets between two pieces of plastic wrap, then lightly bash with a meat mallet or saucepan to flatten them out.

for the breadcrumb mix

Crack the eggs into a bowl, add the milk and whisk together.

In another bowl, combine the breadcrumbs and dukkah. Place the flour on a plate.

Season the pork cutlets with sea salt and freshly ground black pepper, then lightly flour, dusting off any excess flour.

Dip the cutlets into the egg mixture, covering the cutlets completely, then dip them into the spiced crumb mixture.

to cook the cutlets

Place a large frying pan over medium–high heat, with 1 tablespoon of the olive oil and 2 tablespoons of the ghee.

Place one pork cutlet at a time in the pan and cook each side for about 3 minutes until golden brown.

Repeat this process for the remaining cutlets, adding more olive oil and ghee to the pan each time.

Place the cutlets on a tray lined with baking paper and finish in the oven for 12–15 minutes.

Remove the cutlets from the oven and leave to rest for 2–3 minutes.

Meanwhile, bring a saucepan of water to a simmer. Add the salt and blanch the asparagus for 2–3 minutes, then remove with a slotted spoon.

to serve

Place the cutlets on six serving plates and arrange the figs, prosciutto and asparagus alongside. Drizzle with olive oil.

Serve with lemon cheeks and warm béarnaise sauce.

FLANK STEAK SANDWICH

makes 4 sandwiches

method

Season the steaks with sea salt and freshly ground black pepper.

Heat the olive oil in a heavy-based frying pan, or chargrill pan over medium–high heat. Cook the steaks for 4–5 minutes on each side, or until cooked as desired.

Remove from the heat, place on a clean tray and allow the steaks to rest for 5 minutes.

Meanwhile, warm the onion confit in a saucepan.

Slice the bread rolls in half, then place in the hot pan or on the grill, cut side down, until lightly toasted. Turn the rolls over, top each with two cheese slices and grill until just melted.

Spread the bottom half of each roll with 1 tablespoon aïoli. Add some rocket, then top with a steak. Spread 1 tablespoon onion confit over each steak and a dollop of chutney.

Top with the bread lids and serve immediately.

ingredients

4 x 150 g (5½ oz) flank steaks, from wagyu or grain-fed beef
2 tablespoons olive oil
4 tablespoons Onion Confit (see recipe on page 208)
4 Turkish bread rolls
8 thin slices gruyère cheese
4 tablespoons aïoli, or good-quality mayonnaise mixed with a grated garlic clove
rocket (arugula) leaves, to taste
4 tablespoons tomato chutney, or your favourite chutney

SEARED POACHED BEEF FILLET WITH ROASTED CORN & CRISP WITLOF

serves 10

ingredients

2 x 1 kg (2 lb 4 oz) beef fillets, centre
 cut and silver skin removed
500 ml (17 fl oz/2 cups) Veal Stock
 (see recipe on page 195)
extra virgin olive oil, for drizzling
500 ml (17 fl oz/2 cups) hot Madeira
 Sauce (see recipe on page 199)

roasted corn
1 teaspoon sea salt
3 corn cobs

crisp witlof
1½ tablespoons honey
2 teaspoons sherry vinegar
2 tablespoons extra virgin olive oil
5 witlof (chicory), cut in half
1 teaspoon chopped sage
100 g (3½ oz/1⅔ cups) fresh or frozen
 soya beans

method

Season the beef with sea salt and freshly ground black pepper. Heat a large frying pan over high heat, then sear the beef on all sides. Remove from the pan and allow to rest for 5 minutes, then cut each fillet into five even portions.

Place the beef slices in 10 separate small snap-lock bags or cryovac bags. Add 50 ml (1¾ fl oz) of the stock to each bag, then seal.

Place the bags in a large saucepan of rolling water for 6 minutes. Remove from the water and rest the beef in the bags for 3 minutes.

for the roasted corn

Meanwhile, add the salt and corn cobs to a saucepan of simmering water and cook for 5–7 minutes. Remove the corn with tongs and drain.

Season the corn well and place on a hot barbecue or chargrill pan. Cook on all sides for about 5 minutes in total, or until nicely chargrilled.

Place the cobs on a chopping board. Using a sharp knife, cut the corn kernels off so that you have four quarters, but they are still intact as one piece.

for the crisp witlof

Mix the honey and vinegar in a small saucepan with 2 teaspoons water. Simmer until the mixture has reduced down by two-thirds. Set aside.

Add the olive oil to a hot frying pan. Place the witlof in the pan, flat side down. Add the sage and cook the witlof over medium heat for 2–3 minutes, or until golden.

Add the honey and sherry reduction to the pan and cook for a further 30 seconds, then turn the witlof over and cook for another minute. Now add the soya beans and season to taste.

to serve

Open the sealed bags to remove the beef pieces. Slice each beef portion in half, then season and drizzle with olive oil.

Arrange the beef on a serving platter with the corn and witlof. Serve with the madeira sauce.

BARBECUED T-BONE WITH MEDITERRANEAN DRESSING

for the mediterranean dressing

Cut a cross into the base of the tomatoes with a sharp knife. Blanch the tomatoes in boiling water for 5 seconds, then place in an iced water bath to cool. Remove the skins and cut the tomatoes into quarters. Remove the seeds, finely dice the flesh and set aside.

Place a heavy-based saucepan over medium heat. Add the olive oil and shallot and sweat down for 3–5 minutes without browning. Now add the garlic and cook for a further 2–3 minutes, or until tender. Stir in the anchovies and paprika and cook for a further 2 minutes.

Now add the diced tomatoes and cook for 10 minutes, or until the mixture is quite dry. Add the capsicum and cook for 3 minutes or until soft, then add the drained capers and cook for a further 2–3 minutes.

Deglaze the pan with the vermouth, stirring well. Remove from the heat and season with sea salt and freshly ground black pepper.

(The dressing can be made up to 2–3 days ahead. Gently reheat and fold the basil through just before serving.)

Remove the steaks from the refrigerator 30–60 minutes before cooking to ensure they are at room temperature before grilling; this will allow the meat to cook more evenly.

Preheat a barbecue to very high heat for 10–15 minutes with the lid down, to ensure the barbecue is very hot.

Trim off any excess fat from the steaks, but leave on at least one-quarter of the fat, to lock the juices into the meat. Season both sides of the steaks, then sprinkle with the barbecue spice.

Brush the barbecue grill with oil. Scrape the grill clean with a grill brush. Leave one side over high heat and adjust the other side to medium heat.

Sear the steaks over high heat for 2 minutes on each side with the lid down. Now move the steaks to the cooler part of the barbecue and continue grilling with the lid down for 10 minutes for medium-rare, or until cooked as desired.

Rest the steaks for 5–10 minutes before serving.

to serve

Serve the steaks with the Mediterranean dressing, with the zucchini slice alongside.

ingredients

4 T-bone steaks, at least 2.5 cm (1 inch) thick
3 tablespoons barbecue spice
vegetable oil, for brushing
Zucchini Slice (see recipe on page 186), to serve

mediterranean dressing

500 g (1 lb 2 oz) tomatoes
250 ml (9 fl oz/1 cup) extra virgin olive oil
150 g (5½ oz) French shallots, diced
100 g (3½ oz) garlic, chopped
6 anchovies
1 tablespoon smoked paprika
300 g (10½ oz) roasted red capsicum (pepper), peeled and diced
150 g (5½ oz) salted capers, soaked in water overnight, then drained
200 ml (7 fl oz) dry vermouth
4 tablespoons diced basil

WAGYU BRAISED IN BARBECUE SAUCE WITH SHIITAKE & CABBAGE ROLLS

serves 10

braised beef

3 kg (6 lb 12 oz) wagyu or grain-fed beef brisket

6 tablespoons barbecue rub or barbecue spice mix

1 onion, chopped

1 carrot, chopped

2 celery stalks, chopped

150 g (5½ oz) fresh ginger, peeled and sliced

2 garlic cloves, chopped

10 thyme sprigs

5 fresh bay leaves

200 ml (7 fl oz) extra virgin olive oil

200 ml (7 fl oz) port

1 litre (35 fl oz/4 cups) red wine

3 litres (105 fl oz/12 cups) hot Beef Stock (see recipe on page 193)

500 ml (17 fl oz/2 cups) Barbecue Sauce (see recipe below — or use a good-quality Asian barbecue sauce)

sesame oil, to taste

baby coriander (cilantro), to garnish

barbecue sauce

15 Garlic Confit cloves (see recipe on page 208)

750 ml (26 fl oz/3 cups) tomato sauce (ketchup)

3 celery stalks, diced

1½ onions, diced

150 g (5½ oz/¾ cup) soft brown sugar

240 g (8½ oz) unsalted butter

750 ml (26 fl oz/3 cups) worcestershire sauce

250 ml (9 fl oz/1 cup) cider vinegar

3 tablespoons chilli flakes

2 teaspoons cayenne pepper

1 double short black coffee

1 teaspoon ground cloves

10 cinnamon sticks

20 star anise

175 g (6 oz/½ cup) honey

2 tablespoons Tabasco sauce

300 ml (10½ fl oz) liquid smoke (available from barbecue supply stores and specialty spice shops)

cabbage rolls

10 large Chinese cabbage leaves

2 tablespoons olive oil

1 tablespoon grated fresh ginger

1 tablespoon grated garlic

250 g (9 oz) fresh shiitake mushrooms, sliced

250 g (9 oz) oyster mushrooms

50 ml (1¾ fl oz) hoisin sauce

2 tablespoons hot English mustard

for the barbecue sauce

Place all the ingredients in a large saucepan, add 375 ml (13 fl oz/1½ cups) water and mix until well combined. Bring to the boil, reduce the heat and simmer for 30 minutes, or until reduced by about half. Remove from the heat.

Transfer the mixture to a blender and blend until smooth. Pass through a fine sieve.

Allow to cool, then transfer to a clean airtight container. Store in the refrigerator and use as required. The sauce will keep for around 4 weeks.

for the braised beef

Rub the beef with the barbecue rub. Place in a large container with the onion, carrot, celery, ginger, garlic and herbs. Mix well, then cover and marinate in the refrigerator for 24 hours.

The next day, preheat the oven to 140°C (275°F/Gas 1).

Separate the beef and vegetables.

Heat the olive oil in a large flameproof casserole dish over medium–high heat. Brown the beef brisket on all sides, then set aside.

Add the reserved vegetables to the dish, reserving the herbs, and brown them evenly. Stir in the port and wine, simmer until reduced by half.

Add the stock and bring to the boil, then reduce the heat to a simmer. Stir in the barbecue sauce and reserved herbs. Add the beef and bring to a gentle simmer.

Cover with a tight-fitting lid, transfer to the oven and braise for 3–4 hours, or until the beef is tender.

Remove the beef from the braising liquid and place on a tray; reserve the braising liquid. Cover the beef with plastic wrap, place a heavy item on top, then refrigerate until cold.

for the cabbage rolls

While the beef is braising, blanch the cabbage leaves in a saucepan of salted boiling water for 20 seconds. Remove and refresh in ice-cold water, then place on a dry clean cloth.

Heat the olive oil in a frying pan and gently sauté the ginger and garlic until fragrant. Add the mushrooms and sauté for another 3–5 minutes, until tender.

Stir in the hoisin sauce and season with sea salt and freshly ground black pepper. Place the mixture on paper towels to cool.

Take one cabbage leaf and smear a little mustard over it. Place some of the mushroom mixture at one end, like a spring roll. Fold the two sides in, then roll up tight.

Repeat with the remaining cabbage and mushroom mixture. Set the rolls aside.

for the braising sauce

Strain the reserved braising liquid into a clean saucepan. Place over medium heat and simmer until it has reduced by half, ensuring the sauce is not too thick. Remove from the heat and add sesame oil to taste.

to serve

Preheat the oven to 170°C (325°F/Gas 3). Cut the beef into 10 equal portions and place in a roasting tin or on a deep-sided baking tray. Pour the braising sauce over and cover with foil. Reheat for 20 minutes, or until the beef is hot.

Meanwhile, cook the cabbage rolls in a steamer for 8–10 minutes.

Transfer the beef and cabbage rolls to a serving platter, or arrange on 10 plates. Pour some of the braising sauce over, garnish with baby coriander and serve.

PAELLA

serves 6-8

ingredients

800 ml (28 fl oz) Chicken Stock
    (see recipe on page 192)
¼ teaspoon saffron threads
50 ml (1¾ fl oz) extra virgin olive oil
500 g (1 lb 2 oz) chicken wings,
    cut in half
60 g (2¼ oz) chorizo sausage,
    cut into 5 mm (¼ inch) slices
1 onion, chopped
4 French shallots, peeled and
    chopped
2 tablespoons chopped garlic
¼ teaspoon smoked Spanish paprika
220 g (7¾ oz) tin piquillo peppers
    (see note on page 101)
250 g (9 oz) large raw prawns
    (shrimp), peeled and deveined,
    leaving the tails and heads intact
2 lobster tails, split lengthways
    (optional)
4 king crab claws (optional)
330 g (11½ oz/1½ cups) short-grain
    Spanish rice, such as bomba or
    calasparra
3 tablespoons chopped flat-leaf
    (Italian) parsley, plus extra to garnish
2 fresh bay leaves
125 ml (4 fl oz/½ cup) dry white wine
100 g (3½ oz/⅔ cup) fresh peas
12 clams (vongole), scrubbed
12 mussels, scrubbed well, hairy
    beards removed
60 g (2¼ oz) jamón or serrano ham,
    diced
lemon cheeks, to garnish

method

Preheat the oven to 165°C (320°F/Gas 3).

In a saucepan, bring the stock and saffron to a simmer. Leave to simmer for 15 minutes, then set aside.

Heat the olive oil in a metal paella pan measuring 38 cm (15 inches) across the base. Add the chicken wings and fry over high heat for 5 minutes, or until golden on all sides. Remove to a warm platter.

Add the chorizo to the paella pan and sauté for 3 minutes. Add the onion, shallot, garlic and paprika and sauté for 5 minutes, or until the onion is soft. Add the piquillo peppers and cook for 1 minute.

Add the prawns, and the lobster and crab claws, if using. Sauté for a further 3 minutes, or until the prawns and lobster just turn pink.

Transfer the seafood to the platter with the chicken.

Add the rice to the paella pan and stir through. Sprinkle in the parsley and add the bay leaves. Stir in the wine and cook until reduced by half.

Now stir in the hot stock at 2 minute intervals.

Add the peas and season with sea salt and freshly ground black pepper. Bring back to the boil, then reduce the heat to medium. Cook, uncovered, stirring occasionally, for 10–12 minutes.

Bury the prawns and chicken in the rice. Add the clams and the mussels, pushing them into the rice, with the edge that will open facing up. Decorate the paella with the lobster and crab claws, if using.

Transfer to the oven and bake, uncovered, for 15 minutes. Remove from the oven, cover with foil and rest for 5 minutes.

Remove and discard any unopened clams or mussels. Garnish the paella with the ham, lemon cheeks and extra parsley and serve.

STEAMED JEWFISH WITH ORANGE, FETA, DATE & MINT COUSCOUS

serves 4

for the couscous

Bring the orange juice to the boil in a small saucepan. Place the couscous in a large bowl and pour the orange juice over. Tightly cover the bowl with a lid or plastic wrap and leave for 10 minutes. Run a fork through the couscous until light and fluffy.

Thinly slice about two-thirds of the mint and add to the couscous, along with the dates, orange segments and almonds. Crumble the feta over, drizzle with olive oil and the vinegar and mix through well.

Season the fish with sea salt and freshly ground black pepper and place in a steamer. Cover and steam for 7–8 minutes, or until just cooked through.

to serve

Pile the warm or cold couscous onto serving plates and garnish with the remaining whole mint leaves.

Add the fish and drizzle with olive oil to finish.

ingredients

4 x 180 g (6 oz) jewfish fillets or other
  firm white fish fillets, skin on
extra virgin olive oil, for drizzling

couscous

225 ml (7½ fl oz) orange juice
200 g (7 oz/1 heaped cup) instant
  couscous
20 mint leaves
4 dates, pitted and thinly sliced
1 large orange, segmented
  (see note on page 141)
4 tablespoons toasted almonds
150 g (5½ oz) soft marinated feta
  cheese
extra virgin olive oil, for drizzling
2 tablespoons white wine vinegar

BABY CHICKEN BAKED IN SALT & HERB DOUGH

serves 2

ingredients

2 baby chickens, boned (you can ask your butcher to do this for you)

salt and herb dough

800 g (1 lb 12 oz) rock salt, lightly blended
2 kg (4 lb 8 oz) plain (all-purpose) flour
800 ml (28 fl oz) water
3 tablespoons thyme, chopped
3 tablespoons rosemary, chopped
3 tablespoons oregano, chopped
3 tablespoons marjoram, chopped
1 tablespoon freshly ground black pepper
8 free-range egg whites
1 free-range egg, beaten

stuffing

2 tablespoons olive oil
¼ onion, very finely diced
2 garlic cloves, chopped
100 g (3½ oz) Swiss brown mushrooms, sliced
1 bacon rasher, rind removed, finely chopped
½ leek, white part only, washed and thinly sliced
4 dried figs, diced
zest of ½ lemon
2 tablespoons cognac
75 g (2½ oz) chicken livers
500 g (1 lb 2 oz) fresh breadcrumbs
45 g (1½ oz) suet, grated (order ahead from specialty butchers; you can use frozen unsalted butter but it will not give the same flavour)
1 tablespoon flat-leaf (Italian) parsley, chopped
1 free-range egg, lightly beaten

for the stuffing

Heat half the olive oil in a frying pan over medium–high heat. Add the onion and garlic and sauté for a few minutes.

Add the mushrooms, bacon and leek and cook, stirring, for 5 minutes, or until the bacon and mushrooms have browned.

Add the dried figs and lemon zest and deglaze the pan with the cognac, stirring to dissolve any cooked-on bits. Transfer to a large bowl and allow to cool.

Clean the chicken livers by removing the sinew. Sear for 30 seconds on each side in a hot frying pan with the remaining olive oil. Remove from the pan and allow to cool.

Roughly chop the cooled livers and add to the stuffing mixture with the remaining stuffing ingredients. Season with sea salt and freshly ground black pepper and combine well.

Preheat the oven to 200°C (400°F/Gas 6). Wash the chickens and dry thoroughly with paper towels. Place a small mound of the stuffing in the cavity of each chicken, then close the cavity back up again.

for the salt and herb dough

In a bowl, mix together the rock salt, flour, water, herbs, pepper and egg whites to form a dough-like consistency. Divide the dough into four even portions, then roll each one out to a thickness of about 1.5 cm (⅝ inch), using extra flour as required to prevent sticking.

Carefully place a chicken on one piece of the dough. Brush the sides of the dough with the beaten egg, then place another piece of dough over the top of the chicken to cover it completely. Ensure the dough is sealed around the chicken, with no visible holes or tears. Remove any excess dough so that you have a neatly packed chicken.

Repeat this process with the second chicken.

Place the chickens in a roasting tin, seam side down. Transfer to the oven and roast for 30 minutes.

Remove from the oven and allow to rest for 5 minutes.

to serve

Cut around the base of the cooked dough, around each chicken, then pull the top off slowly.

Serve the chickens on a chopping board at the table.

CONFIT DUCK LEGS WITH PANCETTA & MINTED PEAS

serves 6

method

Rub the duck legs on both sides with half the rock salt. Place in a dish and cover with the remaining salt, mixing well. Cover with plastic wrap and place in the refrigerator for 2 hours to cure.

Preheat the oven to 100°C (200°F/Gas ½).

Wash the duck legs in water and pat dry with a clean cloth. Place in a large baking dish and completely cover the legs with the duck or goose fat. Bake for 1 hour 45 minutes, or until the meat starts to come away from the bone.

Remove from the oven and allow to cool.

While the duck is cooling, turn the oven up to 180°C (350°F/Gas 4).

Carefully remove the cooled duck legs from the fat and place on a baking tray lined with baking paper. Place two pancetta rashers over the top of each duck leg.

Return to the oven and bake for 20–25 minutes, or until the pancetta is slightly crisp and the duck legs are hot.

to serve

Place a good spoonful of mushy peas on each serving plate, then place a duck leg on top. Dress with the mint sauce.

Serve with roasted potato mash.

ingredients

6 good-sized duck marylands
500 g (1 lb 2 oz) rock salt
2 kg (4 lb 8 oz) duck fat or goose fat
12 rashers smoked pancetta
Mushy Peas with Mint Sauce
    (see recipe on page 180), to serve
Roasted Potato Mash (see recipe
    on page 179), to serve

TUNA WITH CHIMICHURRI & CORN SALSA

serves 4

ingredients
4 x 200 g (7 oz) tuna steaks
50 ml (1½ fl oz) extra virgin olive oil
dill sprigs, to garnish

corn salsa
3 corn cobs, husks and silks removed
50 ml (1½ fl oz) extra virgin olive oil
6 French shallots, very finely diced
5 garlic cloves
1 red chilli, seeded and very finely
    chopped
2 tablespoons tarragon, chopped
3 tablespoons dill, chopped
3 tablespoons parsley, chopped
zest and juice of 1 lime

chimichurri sauce
100 ml (3½ fl oz) olive oil
1 tablespoon white wine vinegar
½ cup roasted and peeled red
    capsicum (peppers)
1 tablespoon finely chopped garlic
1 tablespoon finely chopped
    red onion
1 teaspoon chilli flakes
1 tablespoon lime juice
3 tablespoons roughly chopped
    coriander (cilantro) leaves
3 tablespoons roughly chopped
    flat-leaf (Italian) parsley

for the corn salsa
Slice the corn kernels from the cobs and set aside.

Place a saucepan over medium heat. Add the olive oil, then add the shallot and garlic and cook for 3 minutes.

Add the chilli and corn kernels and cook, without browning, for 8–10 minutes. Remove from the heat and allow to cool.

Stir in the herbs, lime zest and lime juice and season with sea salt and freshly ground black pepper.

for the chimichurri sauce
Place all the ingredients, except the coriander and parsley, in a blender and blend until smooth. Transfer the mixture to a bowl, stir in the coriander and parsley and set aside.

Drizzle the tuna with the olive oil and season well.

Cook the tuna on a hot barbecue grill or chargrill pan for 2–3 minutes on each side, depending on the thickness of the steaks, just until the tuna is medium-rare.

to serve
Transfer the tuna to four serving plates. Drizzle the chimichurri all around the tuna and top with the corn salsa. Garnish with dill sprigs and serve.

PORK CHOPS WITH BLACK PUDDING, CALVADOS, APPLE & SAGE

serves 4

ingredients

1 pork rack (4 cutlets), skin on
100 g (3½ oz) butter
12 sage leaves
50 g (1¾ oz) sugar
2 apples, peeled, cored and cut
    into wedges
2 tablespoons olive oil
2 good-quality blood sausages,
    thickly sliced
60 ml (2 fl oz/¼ cup) calvados
    (see note)

method

Sprinkle sea salt and freshly ground black pepper over the skin of the pork. Place in a dish, then cover and refrigerate for 3 hours.

Preheat the oven to 220°C (425°F/Gas 7).

Brush the salt off the pork. Place on a greased baking tray and roast for 40 minutes.

Reduce the oven temperature to 160°C (315°F/Gas 2–3) and roast for a further 20 minutes, or until cooked as desired. Remove from the oven, cover with foil and allow to rest.

Meanwhile, heat the butter in a saucepan over medium heat. Add the sage leaves, sugar and apple and cook for 5 minutes, or until soft.

In another saucepan, heat the olive oil over medium heat, then add the sausage slices and cook for 30 seconds on each side. Season with sea salt and freshly ground black pepper.

Add the apple mixture to the sausages, then stir in the calvados and cook for a further 2–3 minutes.

to serve

Cut the pork racks into cutlets and arrange on four serving plates. Spoon the sausage and apple mixture over and serve.

note: Calvados is a dry apple brandy. The finest ones hail from the French region of Normandy, and are aged in oak for at least two years, and up to 40 years.

LAMB CUTLETS WITH BABA GHANOUSH, PISTACHIO TABOULEH & POMEGRANATE

for the pistachio tabouleh

Soak the burghul in warm water for 1 hour. Strain well and place in a bowl.

Season with freshly ground black pepper and add the remaining tabouleh ingredients. Mix well, adding enough olive oil to moisten the mixture. Set aside.

for the baba ghanoush

Pierce the eggplant with a toothpick several times, then wrap it in two layers of foil. Place on a hot barbecue and cook on all sides for about 25 minutes, or until you can feel it collapse when pressed. Remove from the heat and allow to cool slightly.

Unwrap the eggplant, peel the skin off and place the flesh in a colander to drain off any bitter juices.

In a food processor, whiz the tahini, garlic and lemon juice together for 1 minute. With the motor running, add the eggplant, olive oil, sea salt and some freshly ground black pepper. Process until smooth, then place in a serving bowl and set aside.

for the salad

Zest one lemon and set the zest aside. Cut the white pith off the lemon, then remove the skin and pith from the remaining lemon.

Dice the lemons and toss in a bowl with the lemon zest, onion, parsley and pomegranate seeds. Dress with olive oil and set aside.

Cook the cutlets on a hot barbecue grill for 3 minutes on each side for medium, or until cooked to your liking.

Remove from the heat and leave to rest for 5 minutes.

to serve

Arrange the cutlets on a large platter or six serving plates and drizzle with the pomegranate molasses. Serve with the tabouleh, baba ghanoush, salad, flatbread and yoghurt.

ingredients

24 lamb cutlets
150 ml (5 fl oz) pomegranate
    molasses
Lebanese flatbread or Garlic
    Flatbread (see recipe on
    page 22), to serve
plain yoghurt, to serve

baba ghanoush

1 large eggplant (aubergine)
2½ tablespoons tahini
½ teaspoon finely chopped garlic
3 teaspoons lemon juice
1 tablespoon extra virgin olive oil
½ teaspoon sea salt

pistachio tabouleh

100 g (3½ oz/heaped ½ cup) burghul
    (bulgur)
2 cups flat-leaf (Italian) parsley leaves,
    finely chopped
1 cup mint leaves, finely chopped
200 g (7 oz) crushed pistachio nuts
150 g (5½ oz) green olives, pitted and
    chopped
6 Garlic Confit cloves, finely chopped
    (see recipe on page 208)
juice of 1 lemon
extra virgin olive oil, for moistening

salad

2 lemons
1 red onion, sliced into very fine rings
¾ cup flat-leaf (Italian) parsley,
    leaves only
1 pomegranate, halved, the seeds
    collected
extra virgin olive oil, for drizzling

WAGYU SCOTCH MINUTE STEAK WITH ASPARAGUS, TOMATOES, ROASTED VEGETABLES & TRUFFLE JUS

serves 4

method

Preheat the oven to 180°C (350°F/Gas 4).

Peel the parsnip and cut in half widthways. Now cut the smaller end lengthways into quarters or baton shapes, and the larger end into eighths. Place on a baking tray, drizzle with olive oil and season with sea salt and freshly ground black pepper. Roast for 10–15 minutes.

Cut each zucchini in half widthways, then each half lengthways into sixths. Add to the baking tray with the parsnip, drizzle with olive oil and season.

Roast for a further 8–10 minutes, or until both the parsnip and zucchini are tender.

for the truffle dressing

Place the madeira sauce in a saucepan and simmer until the sauce has reduced by two-thirds and has a thick consistency. Remove from the heat and cool slightly.

Whisk in the olive oil, vinegar and the truffle salsa or truffle oil. Season with sea salt and freshly ground black pepper and keep warm.

Season the steaks and cook on a hot barbecue or chargrill pan for 4–5 minutes on each side, or a little longer if you prefer them well done. Remove from the heat and leave to rest for 5 minutes on a wire rack.

Meanwhile, place a saucepan over medium heat. Add 1 tablespoon of olive oil and the asparagus and cook for 2 minutes. Add the cherry tomatoes and cook for 30 seconds, then add the vinegar and cook for 20 seconds. Transfer the mixture to a tray.

Add the roasted parsnip and zucchini to the same tray as the asparagus mixture.

to serve

Place the steaks on four serving plates and arrange the vegetables on top. Drizzle with the truffle dressing.

Scatter the shaved parmesan and chive batons over and serve.

ingredients

1 large parsnip
extra virgin olive oil, for drizzling
    and pan-frying
2 yellow zucchini (courgettes)
4 x 200 g (7 oz) wagyu scotch minute
    steaks or grain-fed beef steaks
8 white asparagus spears, peeled
    and cut in half crossways
20 cherry tomatoes, cut in half
2 tablespoons aged balsamic vinegar
60 g (2¼ oz/⅔ cup) shaved
    parmesan cheese
chive batons, to garnish

truffle dressing

200 ml (7 fl oz) Madeira Sauce
    (see recipe on page 199)
80 ml (2½ fl oz/⅓ cup) olive oil
1 teaspoon cabernet sauvignon
    vinegar or red wine vinegar
20 g (¾ oz) truffle salsa, or 1 teaspoon
    truffle oil (available from select
    delicatessens)

SNAPPER CURRY PIES WITH RAITA & MANGO CHUTNEY

serves 4

ingredients

100 g (3½ oz) chickpeas, soaked in water overnight
1 teaspoon sea salt
700 g (1 lb 9 oz) silverbeet (Swiss chard)
100 g (3½ oz) unsalted butter
8 x 90 g (3¼ oz) snapper fillets, skin on
4 ready-made puff pastry sheets, 30 cm (12 inches) square
2 free-range egg yolks, beaten
Mango Chutney (see recipe on page 209), to serve

yellow curry sauce

5 cloves
2 star anise
1½ cinnamon sticks
2 tablespoons vegetable oil
1 brown onion, chopped
4 garlic cloves, puréed
45 g (1½ oz) fresh ginger, finely grated
1 heaped tablespoon curry powder
1 heaped tablespoon tomato paste (concentrated purée)
1 tablespoon grated palm sugar (jaggery)
5 kaffir lime leaves
zest and juice of 1 lime
300 ml (10½ fl oz) Chicken Stock (see recipe on page 192)
70 g (2½ oz/⅔ cup) coconut milk powder
600 ml (21 fl oz) coconut milk
2 teaspoons soy sauce

raita

250 g (9 oz) labneh, or plain yoghurt strained overnight
1 telegraph (long) cucumber, skin on, seeded, then grated
½ garlic clove, crushed with 1 teaspoon sea salt
15 mint leaves, chopped
juice of ½ lemon
½ teaspoon chaat masala (see note on page 19)

for the yellow curry sauce

Using a spice grinder or a mortar and pestle blend the cloves, star anise and cinnamon sticks until you have a powder. Sift to remove any large pieces, then set aside.

Place a saucepan over medium–high heat and heat the vegetable oil. Add the onion, garlic and ginger. Reduce the heat to medium and cook the onion mixture for 5–10 minutes, or until browned. Stir in the ground spices and the curry powder and cook over low heat for about 5 minutes. Stir in the tomato paste and cook for a further 5 minutes.

Add the palm sugar and turn the heat up slightly, then cook for 5 minutes, or until the sugar has caramelised. Stir in the lime leaves and lime zest.

Meanwhile, heat the stock in a small saucepan.

Whisk the coconut milk powder into the stock, then add to the spices along with the coconut milk and soy sauce. Cook over medium heat for a further 10–15 minutes.

Stir in the lime juice, remove from the heat and leave to cool to room temperature. Strain the chickpeas and place in a saucepan with the salt and enough water to cover. Bring to the boil, then cook over medium heat for 45 minutes, or until the chickpeas are just cooked but still slightly firm. Strain and set aside.

Cut off and discard the white stems from the silverbeet. Rinse the leaves well, drain, then roughly chop.

Place a large saucepan over medium heat. Add the butter and silverbeet, season with sea salt and freshly ground black pepper and cook for 5 minutes, or until the silverbeet has wilted. Remove and place on a tray, then transfer straight to the freezer for 10 minutes, to stop the cooking process.

Remove the silverbeet from the freezer and strain any excess liquid.

for the raita
Mix everything together and keep covered in the refrigerator. The raita can be made 2–3 hours in advance.

Preheat the oven to 180°C (350°F/Gas 4).

Divide the silverbeet and chickpeas among four 18 x 12 cm (7 x 4½ inch) pie containers or ovenproof bowls to form a bed.

Season the snapper fillets and place two pieces in each bowl. Pour 200 ml (7 fl oz) of the yellow curry sauce into each bowl, then cover the bowls with the puff pastry, allowing it to overhang halfway down. Trim the excess pastry.

Brush the egg yolk wash over the pastry. Allow to dry for 5 minutes, then repeat this process twice.

Place the pies on a sturdy baking tray and bake for 15–17 minutes, or until the pastry is golden brown.

Carefully remove the pies from the oven and leave to rest on the tray for 5 minutes before serving.

Serve the pies with the raita and mango chutney.

ROASTED RIB EYE WITH PARSNIP PURÉE, BONE MARROW & MADEIRA JUS

serves 2

ingredients
800 g (1 lb 12 oz) piece of dry-aged, grain-fed rib eye, on the bone, neatly trimmed
1½ tablespoons extra virgin olive oil
baby cress, to garnish

bone marrow and madeira jus
200 g (7 oz) bone marrow (available from good butchers)
2 vine-ripened tomatoes
200 ml (7 fl oz) Madeira Sauce (see recipe on page 199)
6 tarragon sprigs, picked
1 tablespoon baby salted capers, soaked in cold water, then drained

parsnip purée
100 g (3½ oz) unsalted butter
50 ml (1¾ fl oz) extra virgin olive oil
500 g (1 lb 2 oz) parsnips, peeled and thinly sliced
250 ml (9 fl oz/1 cup) thin (pouring) cream

for the bone marrow and madeira jus
Slice the bone marrow and place in a bowl of salted cold water. Cover and soak in the refrigerator for 12 hours.

The next day, preheat the oven to 150°C (300°F/Gas 2).
Season the beef with sea salt and freshly ground black pepper. Add the olive oil to a hot large deep frying pan and quickly seal the beef on all sides, ensuring not to brown too much.
Place the beef on a baking tray and into the oven. Roast for 40–45 minutes, for a rare to medium steak.
Remove from the oven and allow to rest for 5–10 minutes.

for the parsnip purée
While the beef is roasting, place the butter and olive oil in a saucepan over medium–high heat. Add the parsnip, then cover and cook for 10 minutes, or until the parsnip is tender.
Add the cream and continue cooking until the mixture resembles a soft mash.
Scoop the mixture into a food processor and blend until very smooth. Season to taste.

Meanwhile, finish making the bone marrow and madeira jus. Cut a cross into the base of the tomatoes with a sharp knife. Blanch the tomatoes in boiling water for 5 seconds, then place in an iced-water bath to cool. Remove the skins and cut the tomatoes into quarters. Remove the seeds and finely dice the flesh.
Heat the madeira sauce in a saucepan and stir in the diced tomato, tarragon, capers and the drained bone marrow. Season to taste.

to serve
Spoon the parsnip purée onto a serving platter. Slice the beef and arrange over the top.
Drizzle with the hot madeira sauce, garnish with baby cress and serve.

LAMB RUMP WITH SALSA VERDE, CONFIT ONION & ROASTED TOMATOES

serves 4

method

Preheat the oven to 160°C (315°F/Gas 2–3).

Cut the tomatoes in half horizontally and place on a lightly greased baking tray, cut side up. Generously season with sea salt and freshly ground black pepper. Drizzle with 140 ml (4½ fl oz) of the olive oil and bake for 10–15 minutes, or until soft. Remove from the oven and keep warm.

Turn the oven up to 180°C (350°F/Gas 4).

Season the lamb rumps with sea salt. Heat the remaining olive oil in a large ovenproof frying pan over high heat and brown the lamb on both sides.

Transfer the frying pan to the oven and cook the lamb for about 15 minutes for medium-rare. Remove from the oven and allow to rest for 5 minutes.

for the salsa verde

While the lamb is cooking, place all the salsa verde ingredients in a blender and blend until just smooth. Set aside.

to serve

Slice the lamb and arrange on four serving plates. Drizzle the lamb with the salsa verde. Serve with the roasted tomatoes and a spoonful of onion confit.

ingredients

4 large roma (plum) tomatoes
200 ml (7 fl oz) extra virgin olive oil, plus extra for drizzling
4 x 250 g (9 oz) lamb rumps
Onion Confit (see recipe on page 208), to serve

salsa verde

15 sultanas (golden raisins), soaked in port for at least 30 minutes
200 ml (7 fl oz) extra virgin olive oil
1 garlic clove
½ bird's eye chilli, chopped
2 anchovies
1 tablespoon dijon mustard
3 teaspoons capers
4 tablespoons flat-leaf (Italian) parsley, roughly chopped
4 tablespoons mint leaves
4 tablespoons basil leaves
1 teaspoon lemon juice
2 teaspoons cabernet sauvignon vinegar or red wine vinegar
35 ml (1¼ fl oz) warm water

Believe it or not, in my younger days I set out to be a pastry chef — I just loved anything sweet!

As any chef or cook will tell you, desserts and pastries can be some of the trickiest dishes that come out of the kitchen, because you really need to be precise with your measurements.

In my early days working at the Waterside Inn in England, I never really got to work in the pastry section, but it was always amazing to watch the skill and passion of Mr Roux, creating desserts that were truly works of art.

In this chapter I've tried to include a variety of sweets, from whole desserts to biscuits (cookies) and Turkish delight that are perfect with tea or coffee.

I have even included my new and improved signature Salt Liquorice Parfait (page 142) — a popular staple on our Salt grill menu for many years!

DESSERTS

COCONUT PANNA COTTA WITH STAR ANISE-POACHED PEARS & YOUNG COCONUT

serves 10

ingredients
1 young coconut, water reserved
    for making the panna cotta,
    flesh julienned
20 mint leaves, cut into thin strips

ginger confit
50 g (1¾ oz) knob of fresh ginger,
    peeled and very thinly sliced
300 ml (10½ fl oz) Sugar Syrup
    (see recipe on page 204)

coconut panna cotta
150 g (5½ oz/1 cup) grated palm
    sugar (jaggery)
525 ml (18 fl oz) coconut water
5½ titanium-strength gelatine sheets
    (see note), soaked in cold water
    until soft
190 ml (6½ fl oz) coconut cream
190 ml (6½ fl oz) coconut milk

poached pears
500 g (1 lb 2 oz) caster (superfine)
    sugar
10 star anise
2 cinnamon sticks, toasted
2 vanilla beans cut in half lengthways,
    seeds scraped
1 teaspoon ground allspice
10 corella pears

for the ginger confit
Blanch the ginger in a small saucepan of boiling water three times, for 30 seconds each time, to remove any bitterness.

Drain the ginger and transfer to a clean saucepan. Add the sugar syrup and simmer for about 5 minutes.

Remove from the heat and transfer to a clean container. Leave in the refrigerator for a couple of days before using. Julienne and use as required.

for the coconut panna cotta
Place the palm sugar and coconut water in a saucepan and stir over low heat to dissolve the sugar. Add the soaked gelatine and allow to melt. Stir in the coconut cream and coconut milk.

Place the pan over an ice bath, then pour the mixture into ten 90 ml (3 fl oz) dariole moulds or ramekins. Cover with plastic wrap and refrigerate until required.

for the poached pears
Place all the ingredients, except the pears, in a saucepan. Stir in 1.5 litres (52 fl oz/6 cups) water and bring to a simmer.

Peel the pears and leave them whole. Add them to the liquid and poach gently over low heat for 15–20 minutes, or until tender, ensuring not to overcook.

Remove the pears from the poaching liquid and transfer to a tray to cool.

to serve
Turn out each panna cotta into a serving bowl. Arrange a poached pear and some julienned coconut flesh alongside. Garnish with the mint and ginger confit and serve.

note: Titanium-strength gelatine sheets can be purchased from fine food stores.

PASSIONFRUIT & SHEEP'S YOGHURT CHEESECAKE

serves 10

ingredients
5 tablespoons popping candy
     (see note)
10 teaspoons passionfruit powder
     (see note)
silver leaves (see note), to
     garnish

passionfruit sorbet
500 ml (17 fl oz/2 cups)
     passionfruit juice
300 g (10½ oz) bananas, peeled
450 ml (15½ fl oz) Sugar Syrup
     (see recipe on page 204)

biscuit base
70 g (2½ oz) crushed digestive
     biscuits (cookies)
70 g (2½ oz) crushed gingernut
     biscuits (cookies)
50 g (1¾ oz) butter, melted

cheesecake mixture
250 g (9 oz) cream cheese
175 g (6 oz) caster (superfine)
     sugar
375 g (13 oz) sheep's yoghurt
125 g (4½ oz/½ cup) crème
     fraîche
4 titanium-strength gelatine
     sheets (see note on page 132)

passionfruit jellies
500 ml (17 fl oz/2 cups)
     passionfruit juice
200 ml (7 fl oz) orange juice
300 ml (10 fl oz) Sugar Syrup
     (see recipe on page 204)
12 gelatine sheets, soaked in
     cold water until soft

passionfruit sauce
200 ml (7 fl oz) passionfruit juice
100 ml (3½ fl oz) mango purée
1 teaspoon (5 g/⅛ oz) pectin
     (see note)
1 tablespoon sugar
orange juice, if required

for the passionfruit sorbet
Put the passionfruit juice in a blender with the bananas. Whiz to combine, then mix in the sugar syrup and place in an ice-cream maker. Churn until firm and set, then freeze in an airtight container.

(If you don't have an ice-cream maker, the mixture can be poured into a shallow freezer tray. Freeze until almost frozen, then break up the crystals with a fork. Repeat the freezing and forking process a few times.)

for the biscuit base
Mix all the ingredients together and pour into a lined 25 x 12 cm (10 x 4½ inch) tray. Press down to make an even thin layer, then set in the freezer for about 15 minutes.

for the cheesecake mixture
Cream the cream cheese and sugar using a paddle or wooden spoon, making sure there are no lumps.

Using electric beaters, mix in the yoghurt, scraping the bowl regularly, then mix in the crème fraîche. Scrape the bowl again and ensure there are no lumps.

Soak the gelatine sheets in cold water for a few minutes, then gently melt them in a small saucepan with a spoonful of cheesecake mixture, taking care not to let it burn. Stir it back into the cheesecake mixture until smooth.

Pour the mixture over the biscuit base, making sure the top is smooth and flat. Set in the refrigerator for about 2 hours.

for the passionfruit jellies

Line a 17 x 12 cm (6½ x 4½ inch) tray with plastic wrap.

Warm half the passionfruit juice, half the orange juice and half the sugar syrup in a small saucepan. Stir in six of the soaked gelatine sheets. Spread the mixture on the tray and place in the refrigerator to set.

Repeat with the remaining passionfruit juice, orange juice, sugar syrup and gelatine sheets, to make a second jelly mixture. Carefully pour the jelly mixture over the chilled cheesecake and set in the fridge for another hour.

for the passionfruit sauce

In a saucepan, bring the passionfruit juice and mango purée to the boil. Whisk in the pectin mixed with the sugar and cook for 1 minute.

Leave to cool, then adjust the consistency with orange juice if needed.

to serve

Cut the cheesecake into 10 pieces, then place on 10 serving plates.

Cut the remaining passionfruit jelly into rounds using a 2 cm (¾ inch) pastry cutter, then arrange the jellies around the plates.

Add a mound of sorbet to each plate, then decorate each sorbet mound with silver leaf. Sprinkle the popping candy and passionfruit powder around the plates. Dollop the passionfruit sauce around the plates and serve.

note: Popping candy, passionfruit powder, silver leaves and pectin are all available from fine food stores and specialist suppliers.

PEAR & CINNAMON BOMBE ALASKA

makes 10

ingredients
3 large seasonal pears
baby beetroot cress, to garnish

cinnamon ice cream
200 ml (7 fl oz) milk
300 ml (10½ fl oz) thin
    (pouring) cream
1 cinnamon stick, toasted
100 g (3½ oz) caster (superfine)
    sugar
110 g (3¾ oz) free-range
    egg yolks

pear sorbet
250 ml (9 fl oz) pear purée
150 ml (5 fl oz) Sugar Syrup
    for Sorbets (see recipe
    on page 204)

verjuice syrup
250 ml (9 fl oz/1 cup) verjuice
    (see note on page 202)
75 g (2½ oz/⅓ cup) caster
    (superfine) sugar
75 ml (2¼ fl oz) water
30 g (1 oz) knob of fresh ginger,
    peeled and sliced

cinnamon sponge
5 free-range eggs
100 g (3½ oz) sugar
60 g (2¼ oz) plain (all-purpose)
    flour, sifted
a pinch of ground cinnamon

italian meringue
250 g (9 oz) castor (superfine)
    sugar
250 ml (9 fl oz/1 cup) water
5 free-range egg whites
a pinch of cream of tartar

for the cinnamon ice cream
In a saucepan, bring the milk, cream, cinnamon stick and half the sugar to the boil, stirring occasionally. Remove from the heat.

Place the egg yolks and remaining sugar in a bowl and mix together until just combined.

Pour half the milk mixture over the egg mixture and whisk together well.

Pour the mixture back into the pan and heat slowly to 85°C (185°F) on a sugar thermometer.

Pass the mixture through a fine sieve, into a bowl. Cover and chill in the refrigerator until cold.

Transfer the mixture to an ice-cream maker and churn until set. Store in the freezer.

for the pear sorbet
Mix the ingredients together and place in an ice-cream maker. Churn until firm and set, then freeze in an airtight container.

(If you don't have an ice-cream maker, the mixture can be poured into a shallow freezer tray. Freeze until almost frozen, then break up the crystals with a fork. Repeat the freezing and forking process a few times.)

for the verjuice syrup
Bring all the verjuice syrup ingredients to the boil in a saucepan. Remove from the heat and leave to cool completely.

Bring the verjuice syrup back to a simmer. Peel the pears. Using a parisienne scoop or melon-baller, scoop out small balls from the pears and add them to the verjuice syrup. Gently poach the pear balls for 4–6 minutes, or until the pears are just cooked. (This step may be done 1–2 days ahead.)

for the cinnamon sponge

Preheat the oven to 180°C (350°F/Gas 4). Line a 40 x 28 cm (16 x 11¼ inch) baking tray with baking paper

In a bowl, beat the eggs and the sugar until pale and thick, using electric beaters. Fold in the sifted flour and cinnamon.

Spread the mixture over the baking tray and bake for 6–8 minutes, or until firm but springy to the touch. Remove from the oven and allow to cool on the tray.

for the base

Cut 20 circles from the sponge, to fit inside 10 dariole moulds or ramekins, measuring 14 cm (5½ inches) across and 6 cm (2½ inches) deep. Fit one sponge circle inside each mould, to cover the base. Set the other sponge rounds aside.

Half-fill the moulds with the pear sorbet and set in the freezer for 1 hour.

Fill the moulds with the cinnamon ice cream, then cover each one with another round of sponge. Freeze for 2 hours.

De-mould each dessert and place back in the freezer while you make your meringue.

for the Italian meringue

Place the sugar and water in a saucepan. Warm the mixture over medium heat to 121°C (250°F) on a sugar thermometer.

Meanwhile, begin whipping the egg whites and cream of tartar until fluffy, using electric beaters.

Slowly whisk in the sugar syrup in a trickle. Continue whisking until the egg whites have returned to room temperature.

Pile the meringue over the bombes. Place back in the freezer for 20 minutes.

Preheat the oven to 200°C (400°F/Gas 6).

Place the bombes on a baking tray lined with baking paper. Bake for 4–5 minutes, or until the meringue is lightly browned.

to serve

Place each bombe on a separate bowl-plate. Arrange the pear balls around each bombe. Drizzle with the verjuice syrup, garnish with the beetroot cress and serve.

FLOATING ISLANDS

for the meringue

Whisk the egg whites to soft peaks using electric beaters.

Slowly add the sugar and continue beating until all the sugar has been added and the peaks are nice and firm. Fold in the orange zest.

Evenly divide the mixture among six lightly oiled 250 ml (9 fl oz/1 cup) ramekins and cook in a bain-marie for 5 minutes at 160°C (320°F), measured on a sugar thermometer. (If you don't have a bain-marie, use a double-boiler, or a dish set over a saucepan of simmering water.)

for the crème anglaise

In a saucepan, combine the milk, cream and half the sugar over medium–high heat. Bring to the boil, then remove from the heat and set aside.

Mix the egg yolks and remaining sugar together in a metal bowl. Whisk half the hot milk and cream mixture into the egg yolks, then add the remaining hot milk and cream. Whisk well, then transfer to a clean saucepan and place back over the heat, cooking slowly to 75°C (165°F), taking care not to overcook or the eggs will scramble.

Remove from the heat, strain into a clean metal bowl and allow to cool over an ice bath until the mixture is cold. Stir in a good splash of liqueur.

to serve

De-mould the floating islands into six individual serving bowls. Arrange the fruit around the floating islands and drizzle with the crème anglaise.

note: To segment citrus fruit, slice off the top and bottom so it sits flat on the bench. Holding the fruit over a bowl to capture any juices, cut away the peel and bitter white pith using a sharp knife. Now cut diagonally along both sides of each white membrane to remove each segment. Place in a bowl and use as needed.

meringue
4 free-range egg whites
65 g (2½ oz) caster (superfine) sugar
zest of ½ orange

crème anglaise
250 ml (9 fl oz/1 cup) milk
250 ml (9 fl oz/1 cup) thin (pouring) cream
100 g (3½ oz) caster (superfine) sugar
6 free-range egg yolks
Frangelico or other hazelnut liqueur, to taste

mixed fruits (seasonal)
3 fresh figs, sliced
1 peach, flesh sliced
125 g (4½ oz) strawberries, hulled and sliced
125 g (4½ oz/1 cup) raspberries
125 g (4½ oz) blueberries
2 oranges, segmented (see note)
2 ruby grapefruit, segmented (see note)
pulp of 2 passionfruit

SALT LIQUORICE PARFAIT

serves 12

ingredients
1 lime, segmented (see note
    on page 141)

lime jelly
150 ml (5 fl oz) Sugar Syrup
    (see recipe on page 204)
100 ml (3½ fl oz) lime juice
4 titanium-strength gelatine
    sheets (see note on page132),
    soaked in cold water until soft

liquorice tuile
100 g (3½ oz) chopped liquorice
100 ml (3½ fl oz) water

lime syrup
250 g (9 oz) sugar
250 ml (9 fl oz/1 cup) water
juice and zest of 1 lime

liquorice parfait
90 g (3¼ oz) good-quality
    liquorice, chopped
400 ml (14 fl oz) thin (pouring)
    cream
2 free-range eggs
4 free-range egg yolks
100 g (3½ oz) caster (superfine)
    sugar
50 ml (1¾ fl oz) glucose syrup
1 tablespoon Pernod or other
    aniseed-flavoured liqueur

lime chiboust
55 g (2 oz/¼ cup) caster
    (superfine) sugar, plus an
    extra 125 g (4½ oz)
150 g (5½ oz) free-range egg
    yolks
1 tablespoon custard powder
100 ml (3½ fl oz) lime juice
190 ml (6½ fl oz) thin (pouring)
    cream
3 gelatine sheets, soaked in cold
    water until soft
225 g (8 oz) free-range egg whites

for the lime jelly
Warm the sugar syrup and lime juice in a small saucepan and melt in the soaked
gelatine. Transfer to a tray lined with plastic wrap and leave to set in the refrigerator.

for the liquorice tuile
Slowly bring the liquorice and water to a simmer in a small saucepan. Cook until the
liquorice is soft.
    Place in a blender and blend until smooth.
    Spread onto silk mats or baking paper and dry in the oven at 80°C (175°F/Gas ¼)
until dry and crispy; this may take 2–5 hours.

for the lime syrup
Bring the sugar and water to the boil in a small saucepan, stirring until the sugar
has dissolved.
    Remove from the heat and stir in the lime juice and lime zest. Pour into a clean
airtight container and refrigerate until required.

for the liquorice parfait
Place the liquorice and cream in a saucepan and slowly bring to a simmer. Cook for
5 minutes, then blend in a liquidiser or blender while still hot. Transfer to a large bowl
and leave to cool.

Meanwhile, make a thick-ribbon sabayon. Whisk the eggs, egg yolks, sugar, glucose
syrup and Pernod in a heatproof bowl until the sugar has dissolved and the mixture
is combined. Place snugly over a saucepan of gently simmering water (the bowl

should not touch the water) and whisk continuously for 8–10 minutes, or until the mixture is thick, pale and tripled in volume, and holds a ribbon when the whisk is lifted from the mixture. Remove from the heat and whisk for a further 2–3 minutes to prevent the sabayon cooking on the sides of the bowl.

Fold in the cooled liquorice cream mixture to combine, then pour into containers and half freeze; this could take up to 30 minutes.

When half frozen, place the parfait mixture in a piping (icing) bag and pipe large tubes about 30 cm (12 inches) long onto plastic wrap. Roll up and freeze straight away until completely set.

for the lime chiboust

In a bowl, mix together the 55 g (2 oz/¼ cup) sugar, the egg yolks, custard powder and lime juice.

Bring the cream to the boil in a saucepan, remove from the heat, then add the egg yolk mixture. Place back on the heat and simmer until thick.

Stir in the soaked gelatine sheets, remove from the heat and set aside.

Quarter-fill a medium saucepan with water. Set the saucepan over medium heat and bring the water to a simmer.

Combine the egg whites and remaining 125 g (4½ oz) sugar in a heatproof bowl of an electric mixer. Place the bowl over the saucepan and constantly whisk until the sugar has dissolved and the egg whites are warm to the touch — this will take about 3–3½ minutes.

Transfer the bowl to the electric mixer, fitted with the whisk attachment. Now begin whisking, starting on low speed, then gradually increasing to high speed, for about 10 minutes, or until stiff, glossy peaks form.

Add the reserved custard and mix until combined.

Spread the chiboust, 4 mm (⅙ inch) thick, onto a 40 x 28 cm (16 x 11¼ inch) tray lined with baking paper. Place in the freezer for 5 minutes.

Remove from the freezer and place the liquorice parfait tubes in the middle of the chiboust. Roll so that the chiboust covers the liquorice, then place back in the freezer, uncovered, until set.

to serve

Cut the chiboust roll into 3.5 cm (1¼ inch) cylinders. Serve with the lime syrup, lime jelly, lime segments and shards of the liquorice tuile.

RUM, RAISIN & CHOCOLATE BREAD & BUTTER PUDDING

serves 12

ingredients

175 g (6 oz/1 cup) raisins

125 ml (4 fl oz/½ cup) dark rum

8 large croissants, torn into large pieces

100 g (3½ oz) milk or dark chocolate buttons

500 ml (17 fl oz/2 cups) milk

600 ml (21 fl oz) thin (pouring) cream

a pinch of sea salt

2 vanilla beans, cut in half lengthways, seeds scraped

10 free-range eggs

165 g (5¾ oz/¾ cup) caster (superfine) sugar

thick (double) cream or vanilla ice cream, to serve

method

Place the raisins in a small bowl. Pour the rum over. Cover and set aside, at room temperature, for several hours, or overnight.

Drain the raisins, reserving the rum.

Preheat the oven to 150°C (300°F/Gas 2).

Grease a square or round ovenproof dish, measuring at least 5 cm (2 inches) deep and about 25 cm (10 inches) across.

Place a layer of croissant pieces onto the base of the dish, sprinkle with some of the soaked raisins, then some of the chocolate buttons.

Add another layer of croissants, then a little more of the raisins and chocolate. Repeat, reserving a handful of the raisins and chocolate to sprinkle over the top.

Bring the milk, cream, salt, vanilla bean, vanilla seeds and reserved rum to the boil in a saucepan. Remove the saucepan from the heat and discard the vanilla beans. Set aside.

In a large bowl, whisk the eggs and sugar together, then slowly pour in the hot milk mixture, whisking constantly.

Carefully pour the mixture over the croissants, then sprinkle with the reserved raisins and chocolate. Bake for 1 hour, or until the custard has just set.

Serve warm, with thick cream or vanilla ice cream.

ORANGE LAMINGTONS

makes 20

ingredients

8 free-range eggs, separated
2 free-range egg yolks
190 g (6¾ oz) caster (superfine) sugar
80 g (2¾ oz) plain (all-purpose) flour
40 g (1½ oz/⅓ cup) cornflour
    (cornstarch)
zest of 1 orange
40 g (1½ oz) unsalted butter, melted
    and cooled
100 g (3½ oz) desiccated coconut

icing

30 g (1 oz) unsalted butter
125 ml (4 fl oz/½ cup) boiling water
300 g (10½ oz) icing (confectioners')
    sugar, sifted
3 tablespoons orange jelly crystals
juice of 1 orange

method

Preheat the oven to 180°C (350°F/Gas 4). Grease a lamington tin, measuring about 31 x 25 cm (12½ x 10 inches), and about 3 cm (1¼ inches) deep. Line the tin with baking paper.

for the sponge

Beat the 10 egg yolks with 90 g (3¼ oz) of the sugar using electric beaters for 5–10 minutes, or until very pale. Transfer to a large bowl.

Sift the flour and the cornflour three times, then fold into the yolk mixture. Fold in the orange zest.

Beat the egg whites in a separate bowl with the remaining 100 g (3½ oz) sugar for 3–5 minutes, until stiff and glossy.

Fold three-quarters of the egg white mixture into the yolk mixture.

Mix the melted butter with the remaining beaten egg whites until well combined, then fold it into the yolk mixture.

Pour the mixture into the lamington tin and bake for 12–15 minutes, or until golden brown and spongy to the touch.

Remove from the oven and cool in the tin for a few minutes. Turn the sponge out onto a wire rack, cover with a cloth and leave to cool.

for the icing

Melt the butter in the boiling water in a shallow bowl. Pour in the icing sugar and jelly crystals and stir until dissolved. Stir in the orange juice.

to assemble

Spread the coconut on a plate. Cut the sponge into 6 cm (2½ inch) squares.

Dip the sponge squares in the icing, then coat them in the coconut. Place in the fridge for 30 minutes to set the coating.

Lamingtons are best eaten the day they are made.

MOIST ITALIAN APPLE FLAN

for the orange marmalade

Cut the oranges into quarters, leaving the skins on. Place in a saucepan and cover with 500 ml (17 fl oz/2 cups) water. Add the sugar and spices.

Bring to the boil, then reduce the heat and simmer for 40–45 minutes, or until the oranges are very tender.

Remove from the heat and allow to cool. Transfer the oranges to a bowl using a slotted spoon. Strain the syrup to remove the spices.

Return the syrup to the pan and continue to boil gently until the liquid has reduced by half.

Add the oranges to the syrup, then transfer to a blender and blend to a smooth consistency.

for the apple flan

Preheat the oven to 170°C (325°F/Gas 3). Grease a 25 cm (10 inch) spring-form cake tin and line with baking paper.

Place the butter in a small heatproof dish and melt it in the oven, ensuring the butter doesn't burn.

Put the lemon juice and 50 g (1¾ oz) of the sugar in a bowl.

Peel the apples and cut them into thin slices. Add them to the sugar bowl, mix together and set aside.

Break the eggs into a large mixing bowl, add the remaining sugar and beat together until just combined. Add the melted butter, vanilla bean seeds or extract, sifted flour, baking powder and spices. Mix until well combined, then fold the sugar-coated apples through.

Spoon the mixture into the prepared cake tin and sprinkle the pine nuts on top. Bake for 40 minutes, or until a skewer inserted in the centre of the cake comes out clean.

Remove from the oven and leave to cool in the tin for 10 minutes.

for the vanilla cream

Place the cream, icing sugar and vanilla seeds in a mixing bowl. Whisk until soft peaks form, using electric beaters.

to serve

Serve the flan warm, with the orange marmalade and vanilla cream.

orange marmalade
6 oranges
300 g (10½ oz) sugar
3 cinnamon sticks
8 star anise, lightly bashed

apple flan
150 g (5½ oz) unsalted butter
juice of 1 lemon
200 g (7 oz) caster (superfine) sugar
5 apples
5 free-range eggs
1 vanilla bean, cut in half lengthways, seeds scraped (or use a few drops of vanilla extract)
300 g (10½ oz/2 cups) self-raising flour, sifted
1½ teaspoons baking powder
1 teaspoon ground cinnamon
1 teaspoon ground allspice
50 g (1¾ oz/⅓ cup) pine nuts

vanilla cream
300 ml (10½ fl oz) thin (pouring) cream
80 g (2¾ oz) icing (confectioners') sugar
2 vanilla beans, cut in half lengthways, seeds scraped

RASPBERRY MARSHMALLOWS

method

Make a sugar syrup by placing the sugar, glucose and 250 ml (9 fl oz/1 cup) water in a saucepan over medium heat. Warm the mixture up to 118°C (245°F) on a sugar thermometer.

Begin whisking the egg whites to soft peaks using electric beaters.

Now warm the sugar syrup to 121°C (250°F), then remove the pan from the heat. Stir in the gelatine and mix until it has dissolved.

Slowly add the sugar syrup to the whisked egg whites in a trickle, whisking until all the sugar syrup has been used. Continue whisking until the egg whites have returned to room temperature.

When the mixture has cooled, add the raspberry compound and whisk through well.

Pour into a 20 x 12 cm (8 x 4½ inch) tray lined with plastic wrap. Cover and chill in the refrigerator overnight.

When ready to serve, cut into squares and roll in the sugar décor.

note: Raspberry compound is a fruit concentrate and is available from fine food stores.

ingredients

500 g (1 lb 2 oz) sugar

45 ml (1½ fl oz) glucose syrup

150 g (5½ oz) free-range egg whites

25 g (1 oz) titanium-strength gelatine sheets (see note on page 132), soaked in cold water until soft, then squeezed of excess water

2 tablespoons raspberry compound (see note)

sugar décor, or equal quantities of cornflour (cornstarch) and icing (confectioners') sugar, for dusting

COCONUT RICE PUDDING WITH MANGO SORBET

serves 8

ingredients
1 mango, peeled and sliced
baby coriander (cilantro)
    leaves, to garnish

coconut rice pudding
400 ml (14 fl oz) coconut milk
270 ml (9½ fl oz) coconut
    cream
335 ml (11¼ fl oz/1⅓ cups) milk
1 vanilla bean, cut in half
    lengthways, seeds scraped
180 g (6 oz) arborio rice
90 g (3¼ oz) caster (superfine)
    sugar
2 free-range egg yolks
45 g (1½ oz) sugar

mango sorbet
500 ml (17 fl oz) mango purée
300 ml (10½ fl oz) Sugar Syrup
    (see recipe on page 204)

palm sugar syrup
125 g (4½ oz) grated palm
    sugar (jaggery)
150 ml (5 fl oz) water
½ lemongrass stem
juice of ½ lime

cigar tuiles
125 g (4½ oz) unsalted butter
150 g (5½ oz) icing
    (confectioners') sugar, sifted
½ vanilla bean, cut in half
    lengthways, seeds scraped
90 g (3¼ oz) free-range egg
    whites
115 g (4 oz) plain (all-purpose)
    flour

rice pudding foam (optional)
125 g (4½ oz) rice pudding
    (from the Coconut Rice
    Pudding recipe, left)
150 ml (5 fl oz) thin (pouring)
    cream

for the coconut rice pudding
Combine the coconut milk, coconut cream and milk in a saucepan. Add the split vanilla bean and the vanilla seeds and bring to the boil.

Stir in the rice, reduce the heat to a simmer and slowly cook for 30–40 minutes, or until the mixture is soft and thick.

Take the saucepan off the heat, stir in the caster sugar and allow to cool for 15 minutes.

While the rice pudding is cooling, make a sabayon. Whisk the egg yolks and sugar in a heatproof bowl until the sugar has dissolved and the mixture is combined. Place snugly over a saucepan of gently simmering water (the bowl should not touch the water) and whisk continuously until the mixture is thick, pale and holds a ribbon when the whisk is lifted from the mixture. Remove from the heat and whisk for a further 2–3 minutes to stop the sabayon cooking on the sides of the bowl.

Fold the sabayon through the rice pudding. Transfer to an airtight container and refrigerate for 24 hours.

for the mango sorbet
Mix the mango purée and sugar syrup together and place in an ice-cream maker. Churn until firm and set, then freeze in an airtight container.

(If you don't have an ice-cream maker, the mixture can be poured into a shallow freezer tray. Freeze until almost frozen, then break up the crystals with a fork. Repeat the freezing and forking process a few times.)

for the palm sugar syrup

In a saucepan, bring the palm sugar, water and lemongrass to the boil. Reduce the heat and simmer until reduced to a syrup. Allow to cool, then stir in the lime juice.

for the cigar tuiles

Preheat the oven to 160°C (315°F/Gas 2–3).

Mix the butter, icing sugar and vanilla seeds until pale using electric beaters. Beat in the egg whites, then fold in the flour.

Cut a piece of plastic (an ice-cream lid is ideal) into a 13 x 9 cm (5 x 3½ inch) rectangle. Cut a rectangle 10 x 6 cm (4 x 2½ inch) out of the middle, so it resembles a frame. Place the plastic frame on a silk mat or a sheet of baking paper and scrape an eighth of the tuile mixture over, to cover the centre of the frame. Remove the frame, leaving the tuile mixture on the mat. Repeat three times.

Place the four tuiles on a baking tray and bake for 4–6 minutes, or until the tuile is lightly brown. Remove from the oven.

Roll each tuile around a wooden spoon handle. Carefully remove the tuile and allow to cool.

Repeat this process to get eight tuiles in total.

for the rice pudding foam (optional)

In a saucepan, warm up the rice pudding and cream. Transfer to a blender and blend until smooth.

Place the mixture into a creamer. Add one creamer gas cartridge and fill the tuiles with the rice foam mixture.

to serve

Place a few tablespoons of the rice pudding around each plate, then arrange the mango slices and tuiles around each plate.

Add a few scoops of mango sorbet to each plate and drizzle with the palm sugar syrup. Garnish with baby coriander leaves and serve.

CHOCOLATE SELF-SAUCING PUDDING

serves 4

ingredients

100 g (3½ oz) unsalted butter, melted
125 ml (4 fl oz/½ cup) milk
1 free-range egg
150 g (5½ oz/1 cup) self-raising flour
1 tablespoon unsweetened cocoa
    powder
110 g (3¾ oz/½ cup) caster (superfine)
    sugar
60 g (2¼ oz) dark chocolate, roughly
    chopped
lightly whipped cream, to serve

topping

1 tablespoon unsweetened cocoa
    powder
220 g (7¾ oz/1 cup firmly packed)
    soft brown sugar
500 ml (17 fl oz/2 cups) boiling water

method

Preheat the oven to 180°C (350°F/Gas 4).

In a large bowl, combine the butter, milk and egg.

In a separate bowl, sift the flour and cocoa together, then stir in the sugar and chocolate.

Gradually add the flour mixture to the wet ingredients and mix well. Spoon into either four individual pudding basins (moulds), about 400 ml (14 fl oz) each, or one large pudding basin, about 1.5 litres (52 fl oz/6 cups) in capacity.

for the topping

Combine the cocoa and sugar and sprinkle over the pudding mixture.

Gently pour 125 ml (4 fl oz/½ cup) of the boiling water over each individual pudding, or the whole 500 ml (17 fl oz/2 cups) boiling water over the single large pudding.

Cover the pudding or puddings with lids, or loosely cover with foil. Place on a baking tray, to catch any overflow of the mixture.

Bake for 30 minutes for the individual puddings, and about 45 minutes if making one large pudding. The puddings should be cooked until firm to the touch.

Serve immediately, with lightly whipped cream.

MALAKOFF

method

Melt the chocolates together over a bain-marie. (If you don't have a bain-marie, use a double-boiler, or a bowl set over a saucepan of simmering water.)

Remove from the heat and fold in the remaining ingredients.

Pour the mixture onto a 20 x 12 cm (8 x 4½ inch) tray lined with baking paper. Leave uncovered and allow to chill in the refrigerator for about 3 hours.

When ready to serve, cut to the desired size and serve.

note: You'll find praline paste in fine food stores.

ingredients

300 g (10½ oz) dark chocolate
200 g (7 oz) white chocolate
300 g (10½ oz) praline paste
   (see note)
100 g (3½ oz/⅔ cup) currants
50 g (1¾ oz/⅓ cup) pistachio nuts
50 g (1¾ oz) hazelnuts
50 g (1¾ oz/⅓ cup) almonds

TURKISH DELIGHT

makes 1 tray

method

Combine the sugar and lemon juice in a saucepan. Stir until the sugar has dissolved and cook until the mixture has reached 121°C (250°F) degrees on a sugar thermometer. Remove from the heat.

Mix the cornflour and rosewater together until smooth, then add to the sugar syrup. Add a few drops of food colouring and mix well.

Bring to the boil and cook for 3–5 minutes, until the mixture is thick.

Remove from the heat and allow the mixture to cool a little. Mix the gelatine through.

Pass the mixture through a fine sieve and pour onto a 20 x 12 cm (8 x 4½ inch) tray lined with baking paper. Cover and refrigerate overnight.

Next day, remove from the refrigerator and cut into squares using a hot knife. Dust with the sugar décor and serve.

Turkish delight will keep in an airtight container in the fridge for up to 1 week.

ingredients

500 g (1 lb 2 oz) caster (superfine)
   sugar
100 ml (3½ fl oz) lemon juice
65 g (2½ oz/½ cup) cornflour
   (cornstarch)
90 ml (3 fl oz) rosewater
a few drops of red food colouring
22 g (¾ oz) titanium-strength gelatine
   sheets (see note on page 132),
   soaked in cold water until soft
sugar décor, or equal quantities of
   cornflour (cornstarch) and icing
   (confectioners') sugar, for dusting

MINI LEMON TARTS

makes 25

ingredients
25 tart shells, each 4 cm (1½ inches),
    made using Sweet Pastry (see
    recipe on page 205), and cooked
    according to the Tart Shells
    instructions on page 206

lemon curd
100 g (3½ oz) butter
90 ml (3 fl oz) lemon juice
85 g (3 oz) sugar
85 g (3 oz) free-range egg yolks

meringue
100 g (3½ oz) caster (superfine) sugar
50 g (1¾ oz) free-range egg whites

for the lemon curd
In a saucepan, bring the butter, lemon juice and half the sugar to the boil, stirring occasionally.

Mix the egg yolks in a mixing bowl with the remaining sugar. Pour in the butter mixture and whisk to combine.

Return the mixture to the saucepan and cook, without boiling, for 5–7 minutes, or until the mixture becomes thick.

Transfer to a bowl, cover and refrigerate for 3 hours.

for the meringue
Place the sugar and 1½ tablespoons water in a saucepan over medium heat and stir until the sugar has dissolved. Warm the mixture to 121°C (250°F) on a sugar thermometer.

Meanwhile, whip the egg whites using electric beaters until fluffy.

Slowly add the sugar syrup to the whisked egg whites in a trickle, whisking until all the sugar syrup has been used. Continue whisking until the egg whites have returned to room temperature.

Place the mixture in a piping (icing) bag.

Remove the lemon curd from the refrigerator and place in a separate piping bag.

Pipe the mixture into the tart shells, then pipe the meringue on top to resemble a soft-serve ice cream.

Lightly brown the meringue topping using a kitchen blow torch, or under a hot oven grill (broiler). Serve immediately.

LEMON SUNSHINE PUDDING

method

Preheat the oven to 150°C (300°F/Gas 2).

Beat the egg yolks and the 125 g (4½ oz) sugar in a bowl until light and creamy, using electric beaters.

Beat in the milk, lemon juice and lemon zest, then fold in the flour.

In a separate bowl, beat the egg whites until soft peaks form. Add the extra 1 tablespoon sugar and beat until the sugar has dissolved.

Fold the egg whites into the lemon mixture, then pour into a greased 2 litre (70 fl oz/8 cup) casserole dish, or four 300 ml (10½ fl oz) individual moulds.

Stand the dish or dishes in a shallow pan of cold water. Carefully transfer to the oven and bake for 40 minutes.

Turn the oven up to 160°C (315°F/Gas 2–3) and bake for a further 10 minutes, or until the pudding is lightly golden in colour.

Remove from the oven and place the casserole dish or individual moulds on a napkin-lined platter or plates.

Serve with vanilla ice cream.

ingredients

3 free-range eggs, separated

125 g (4½ oz) caster (superfine) sugar, plus 1 tablespoon extra

250 ml (9 fl oz/1 cup) milk

juice of ½ lemon

1 tablespoon grated lemon zest

1 tablespoon self-raising flour, sifted

vanilla ice cream, to serve

BERRY FOOL

serves 6

ingredients

250 g (9 oz) strawberries, hulled
250 g (9 oz) blueberries
250 g (9 oz) raspberries
2 tablespoons lemon juice
75 g (2½ oz/⅓ cup) caster (superfine)
    sugar
400 ml (14 fl oz) thin (pouring) cream
1½ tablespoons icing (confectioners')
    sugar
100 g (3½ oz) milk chocolate, shaved
    (optional)

method

Place the berries, lemon juice and sugar in a medium saucepan. Stir and bring to the boil.

Turn the heat down and simmer gently, uncovered, for 5 minutes. Remove from the heat and leave to cool.

Use a hand-held blender or food processor to coarsely purée the mixture.

Place the cream and icing sugar in a large bowl and beat using electric beaters until soft peaks form.

Gently stir the berry mixture through the cream to create a 'ripple' effect. Cover and refrigerate for 1–1½ hours.

To serve, spoon into bowls and top with shaved chocolate, if desired.

BAILEYS CHOCOLATE TRUFFLE

makes 25

ingredients

200 ml (7 fl oz) thick (double) cream
300 g (10½ oz) milk chocolate,
    chopped
50 ml (1¾ fl oz) Baileys Irish Cream
unsweetened cocoa powder,
    for dusting

method

In a saucepan, bring the cream to the boil.

Place the chocolate in a bowl, pour the hot cream over and whisk well until the chocolate has melted. Add the Baileys and mix until combined.

Cover and chill in the refrigerator for 3–4 hours.

Using a teaspoon, roll the chilled mixture into balls.

Spread the cocoa on a tray and roll the chocolate truffles around until coated.

Place the truffles on a clean tray. Cool for 10 minutes in the refrigerator before serving.

CHOCOLATE PANFORTE

method

Preheat the oven to 160°C (315°F/Gas 2–3).

Line a 2 cm (¾ inch) deep, 29 x 19 cm (11½ x 7½ inch) cake tin or baking tray with baking paper.

In a large bowl, mix together all the ingredients except the honey, sugar, chocolate and icing sugar.

In a saucepan, bring the honey and sugar to the boil, then add the dark chocolate, stirring until melted.

Pour the hot mixture into the dry ingredients and stir well; if the mixture is too dry, add 1–2 tablespoons water, ensuring the mixture is very sticky. Stir until well combined.

Press the mixture into the prepared tin and bake for 1 hour, or until the top of the loaf feels spongy to the touch.

Remove from the oven and leave to cool completely in the tin. Turn the panforte out onto a chopping board, removing the baking paper.

To serve, cut the panforte into small squares, rectangles or diamonds and dust with icing sugar.

ingredients

100 g (3½ oz) dried figs, chopped

75 g (2½ oz/⅓ cup) finely chopped glacé ginger

100 g (3½ oz) mixed peel (mixed candied citrus peel)

200 g (7 oz) hazelnuts

125 g (4½ oz) macadamia nuts

225 g (8 oz/1½ cups) plain (all-purpose) flour

4 tablespoons unsweetened cocoa powder

½ teaspoon ground cinnamon

½ teaspoon ground cloves

150 ml (5 fl oz) honey

200 g (7 oz) caster (superfine) sugar

125 g (4½ oz) dark chocolate

icing (confectioners') sugar, for dusting

CHURROS WITH ORANGE MARMALADE & CHOCOLATE SAUCE

serves 4–6

ingredients

1 quantity Orange Marmalade
(see Moist Italian Apple Flan
recipe on page 147)
1 quantity Vanilla Cream
(see Moist Italian Apple Flan
recipe on page 147)

churros

190 ml (6½ fl oz) water
60 ml (2 fl oz/¼ cup) orange juice
125 g (4½ oz) butter
a pinch of sea salt
250 g (9 oz/1⅔ cups) plain
(all-purpose) flour
5 free-range eggs
vegetable oil, for deep-frying

cinnamon sugar

3 tablespoons caster (superfine) sugar
1 tablespoon ground cinnamon

chocolate sauce

150 ml (5 fl oz) thin (pouring) cream
150 g (5½ oz) dark chocolate,
chopped

for the churros

In a saucepan, bring the water, orange juice, butter and salt to the boil. Reduce the heat to low, then mix in the flour and cook down until there are no lumps.

Transfer to a mixing bowl. Using a paddle or wooden spoon, start mixing until the mixture is warm.

Mix in two eggs, then another two eggs, then the final egg, and continue mixing until the consistency is soft enough to pipe.

Transfer the mixture to clean containers, cover with plastic wrap and store in the refrigerator for 2 hours.

(The churros mixture is best made to serve the same day, but can be made up to one day in advance.)

Fill a deep-fryer or large heavy-based saucepan one-third full of vegetable oil and heat the oil to 180°C (350°F), or until a cube of bread dropped into the oil turns golden brown in 15 seconds.

Spoon the churros mixture into a piping (icing) bag fitted with a medium nozzle.

Pipe medium to long tubes of the mixture into the deep-fryer and cook for about 2 minutes. Flip the churros over and cook for a further 2 minutes, or until golden brown.

Drain on paper towels and repeat with the remaining churros mixture.

for the cinnamon sugar

Combine the sugar and cinnamon together on a tray, then roll the hot churros through the mixture.

for the chocolate sauce

Bring the cream to a simmer in a saucepan. Add the chocolate, remove from the heat and stir until melted.

to serve

Serve the hot churros with the chocolate sauce, vanilla cream and orange marmalade.

PEACH TART WITH MASCARPONE

serves 4

ingredients

1 litre (35 fl oz/4 cups) Sugar Syrup
    (see recipe on page 204)
1 vanilla bean, cut in half lengthways,
    seeds scraped
juice of 2 limes
3 peaches, halved and stoned
4 free-range eggs, separated
60 g (2¼ oz) sugar
500 g (1 lb 2 oz) mascarpone cheese
icing (confectioners') sugar, for dusting
4 small tart shells, each 10 cm
    (4 inches), made using Sweet
    Pastry (see recipe on page 205),
    and cooked according to the
    Tart Shells instructions on page 206

method

Place the sugar syrup in a saucepan with the vanilla bean and vanilla seeds. Add the lime juice and peach halves and bring to a simmer. Cook for 5–8 minutes, or until tender but still a little firm.

Remove from the heat. Using a slotted spoon, remove the peaches to a bowl or container. Allow the syrup to cool.

Pour the cooled syrup over the peaches. Cover and refrigerate for 24 hours to infuse.

In a bowl, beat the egg yolks and two-thirds of the sugar until pale, using electric beaters. Slowly beat in the mascarpone.

In a separate bowl, whisk the egg whites with the remaining sugar until firm peaks form, then fold in the mascarpone mixture to combine.

to assemble

Peel away the skin from the peaches. Cut the peach halves into quarters and dust them with icing sugar.

Glaze the peaches with a kitchen blow torch, or under a hot oven grill (broiler).

Place a tart shell in the middle of each serving plate and fill the shells with the mascarpone mixture.

Arrange one-quarter of the peach slices on top of each tart, then drizzle the peach syrup on and around each tart and serve.

VANILLA CRÈME BRÛLÉE WITH BISCOTTI

serves 4

for the crème brûlée

Heat the milk, cream and half the sugar in a saucepan.

Add the vanilla beans and vanilla seeds, then remove the pan from the heat just before the mixture reaches boiling point. Allow the mixture to cool slightly.

While the mixture is still warm, mix the egg yolks with the remaining sugar in a separate bowl until combined. Stir the egg yolk mixture into the milk and cream mixture.

Pass through a sieve and cover with plastic wrap. Store in the refrigerator overnight.

The next day, preheat the oven to 100°C (200°F/Gas ½).

Remove the crème brûlée mixture from the refrigerator and stir well. Evenly pour the mixture into four 220 ml (7½ fl oz) brûlée dishes. Place on a baking tray, transfer to the oven and bake for 30 minutes. Turn the baking tray around and check every 5–10 minutes during cooking. The custards should be fully set, with no bubbles.

Remove from the oven and allow the brûlée dishes to cool at room temperature.

Just before serving, sprinkle 1½ tablespoons of the demerara sugar over each crème brûlée. Evenly blast the topping using a kitchen blow torch. (Scorching them under an oven grill/broiler won't work.)

Serve with biscotti.

ingredients

6 tablespoons demerara sugar
Biscotti (see recipe on page 172), to serve

crème brûlée

330 ml (11¼ fl oz/1⅓ cups) milk
330 ml (11¼ fl oz/1⅓ cups) thin (pouring) cream
140 g (5 oz/⅔ cups) sugar
3 vanilla beans, cut in half lengthways, seeds scraped
140 g (5 oz) free-range egg yolks

TOFFEE SOUFFLÉS WITH PECAN BUTTER ICE CREAM

serves 6

dark toffee
300 g (10½ oz) caster
  (superfine) sugar
100 ml (3½ fl oz) water

caramelised pecans
500 g (1 lb 2 oz/5 cups) pecans
300 g (10½ oz) sugar

caramelised condensed milk
395 g (13¾ oz) tin condensed
  milk

pecan butter ice cream
300 ml (10½ fl oz) milk
450 ml (16 fl oz) thin (pouring)
  cream
½ vanilla bean, cut in half
  lengthways, seeds scraped
160 g (5½ oz) sugar
160 g (5½ oz) free-range egg
  yolks

soufflé base
150 g (5½ oz) Dark Toffee
  (from the Dark Toffee
  recipe, left)
400 ml (14 fl oz) skim milk
40 g (1½ oz/⅓ cup) cornflour
  (cornstarch), whisked
  smooth with an extra
  2 tablespoons skim milk

toffee soufflé
400 g (14 oz) Soufflé Base
  (from the Soufflé Base
  recipe, left)
a splash of butterscotch liqueur
200 g (7 oz) free-range egg
  whites
100 g (3½ oz) sugar

for the dark toffee
Place the sugar and water in a saucepan over medium heat. Cook, without burning, until dark in colour.

Remove from the heat and pour onto a regular-sized tray to cool.

When cool, bash the tray against the bench to break up the toffee and transfer the pieces to an airtight container.

The toffee can be made a few days ahead.

for the caramelised pecans
Preheat the oven to 170°C (325°F/Gas 3).

Place the pecans on a baking tray and roast in the oven for 4–5 minutes. Remove from the oven.

Place the sugar in a saucepan and cook over medium heat, without stirring, until the sugar begins to turn a dark rich colour. If the sugar is not dark, the caramel will not be strong enough.

Add the roasted pecans and stir, ensuring they are well coated with the caramel. Remove from the heat and pour onto a tray lined with baking paper to cool. Roughly chop the pecans and store in an airtight container.

for the caramelised condensed milk

Three-quarters fill a saucepan with water and bring to a simmer.

Remove the wrapper from the tin of condensed milk and place the tin in the water. Cook for 8 hours, topping the water as the level gets low.

Remove the tin and cool to room temperature.

Open the tin and spoon the caramel into a clean bowl. Cover and set aside.

(This element can be made 2–3 days in advance and stored in the fridge.)

for the pecan butter ice cream

In a saucepan, bring the milk, cream, vanilla bean, vanilla seeds and half the sugar to the boil.

Whisk the egg yolks with the remaining sugar in a heatproof bowl. Whisk in half the hot milk and cream mixture. Whisk in the remaining hot milk and cream mixture and pour into a clean saucepan. Place back over the heat and slowly cook to 85°C (185°F).

Place the mixture in an ice-cream maker and churn until the ice cream has just set.

Add the chopped caramelised pecans and caramelised condensed milk and mix to create swirls.

Transfer to a clean container and place in the freezer until required.

for the soufflé base

Place the toffee pieces in a saucepan. Add the skim milk and gently melt the toffee over low heat until dissolved, stirring occasionally.

Bring the caramel to the boil, then stir in the cornflour mixture. Reduce the heat and simmer for 5–8 minutes, until nice and thick. Remove from the heat and transfer to a clean container.

Cover with plastic wrap and refrigerate for about 2 hours.

The soufflé base can be made a day in advance.

for the toffee soufflé

Preheat the oven to 180°C (350°F/Gas 4).

Whisk the soufflé base and liqueur together until smooth.

Begin whisking the egg whites using electric beaters until they start to fluff up, then slowly add the sugar and whisk until you have firm peaks.

Fold one-third of the egg whites into the soufflé base, then very gently fold in the remaining egg whites.

Pour into six pots or soufflé moulds, measuring about 9 cm (3½ inches) across and 6 cm (2½ inches) deep.

Place on a baking tray and bake for 9–10 minutes, or until risen sufficiently.

Serve immediately, with the pecan butter ice cream.

RASPBERRY & CHOCOLATE FRANGIPANE TART

serves 8–10

for the white chocolate cream

Put the chocolate in a heatproof bowl.

Heat the milk and honey in a saucepan and stir until the honey has dissolved. Stir in the gelatine, then pour the mixture over the chocolate. Stir until the chocolate has melted and the ganache is smooth.

Allow to cool, then fold in the whipped cream.

This mixture can be made a day in advance; cover and keep in the fridge until required.

for the tart shells

Roll out the pastry with a rolling pin. Line a buttered 22 cm (8½ inch) flan (tart) tin with the pastry, then leave to rest in the refrigerator for 20 minutes.

Meanwhile, preheat the oven to 160°C (315°F/Gas 2–3).

Place a sheet of baking paper over the tart. Cover with some dried rice or beans and blind-bake the pastry for 8–12 minutes, or until the edge of the tart begins to colour.

Remove the rice or beans and baking paper and bake for a further 8–12 minutes, or until the base is cooked.

Remove from the oven and leave the tart shell to cool in the tin, at room temperature.

for the tart filling

While the tart is cooling, mix the eggs, egg yolk, sugar and almond meal together in a bowl. Stir in the melted butter, then the cream.

Heat the oven to 160°C (315°F/Gas 2–3).

Spread the chopped chocolate in the bottom of the cooled tart. Scatter with the raspberries, then pour the tart filling over the strawberries.

Bake for 35–40 minutes, or until the pastry is golden. Remove from the oven and leave to rest in the tin for 10 minutes.

Remove the tart from the tin, then cut into wedges. Serve with the white chocolate cream.

ingredients

300 g (10½ oz) Sweet Pastry (see recipe on page 205); use about two-thirds of the quantity

100 g (3½ oz) white chocolate, chopped

200 g (7 oz) raspberries

white chocolate cream

75 g (2½ oz) white chocolate, chopped

75 ml (2¼ fl oz) milk

2 teaspoons honey

1 titanium-strength gelatine sheet (see note on page 132), soaked in cold water until soft, then squeezed of excess water

100 ml (3½ fl oz) thickened (whipping) cream, whipped into soft peaks

tart filling

3 free-range eggs

1 free-range egg yolk

1¾ tablespoons caster (superfine) sugar

75 g (2½ oz) almond meal

50 g (1¾ oz) butter, melted

200 ml (7 fl oz) thin (pouring) cream

AFFOGATO

serves 8

ingredients
espresso coffee, to serve
Frangelico, Amaretto or
    Licor 43, to serve

vanilla ice cream
300 ml (10½ fl oz) milk
450 ml (16 fl oz) thin (pouring)
    cream
1 vanilla bean, cut in half
    lengthways, seeds scraped
165 g (5¾ oz/¾ cup) caster
    (superfine) sugar
160 g (5½ oz) free-range egg
    yolks

hazelnut praline cream
240 g (8½ oz) free-range egg
    yolks
100 g (3½ oz) caster (superfine)
    sugar
90 g (3¼ oz/⅔ cup) custard
    powder
1 litre (35 fl oz/4 cups) milk
500 g (1 lb 2 oz) hazelnut
    praline

hazelnut macaroons
100 g (3½ oz) icing
    (confectioners') sugar
100 g (3½ oz) hazelnut meal
100 g (3½ oz) caster (superfine)
    sugar
50 ml (1½ fl oz) water
40 g (1½ oz) free-range egg
    whites

for the vanilla ice cream
Place the milk, cream, vanilla bean and vanilla seeds in a saucepan with half the sugar. Stir to dissolve the sugar and bring to the boil.

Meanwhile, combine the egg yolks and remaining sugar in a bowl.

Remove the milk and cream mixture from the heat and pour half into the egg mixture. Whisk well, then continue to pour in the remaining cream mixture and whisk through until well combined.

Return the mixture to the saucepan and slowly warm to 85°C (185°F) on a sugar thermometer.

Transfer to a bowl, then cover and cool in the refrigerator.

When the mixture is cold, pass through a sieve and churn in an ice-cream maker.

for the hazelnut praline cream
Whisk the egg yolks, sugar and custard powder together in a mixing bowl. Whisk in the milk until smooth, then transfer to a clean saucepan.

Place the saucepan over medium heat and cook for 10–15 minutes, until the mixture has thickened. Remove from the heat, add the hazelnut praline and mix through well.

Pour the mixture onto a clean tray, lightly cover with plastic wrap and chill in the fridge until completely cold.

for the hazelnut macaroons
Preheat the oven to 170°C (325°F/Gas 3).

Sift the icing sugar and hazelnut meal together into a bowl.

Now make an Italian meringue by placing a small saucepan over low heat. Add the sugar and water, then swirl the pan over the heat to dissolve the sugar completely — do not stir. Increase the heat and boil to 115°C (240°F), using a sugar thermometer for accuracy.

Wash down the inside of the pan with a wet pastry brush, to help prevent sugar crystals forming around the side.

Meanwhile, using an electric mixer, whip the egg whites on low speed until foamy. Increase the speed to medium and beat until soft peaks form.

With the mixer running, pour the hot sugar syrup in a thin stream over the fluffed egg whites. Continue beating until the egg whites are stiff and glossy and the mixture has cooled to room temperature.

Fold the sifted icing sugar mixture through the meringue and place in a piping (icing) bag. Pipe the mixture into 3 cm (1¼ inch) discs, onto a baking tray lined with silk mats or baking paper.

Bake the meringues for 20 minutes. Switch off the oven, leaving the baking tray in the oven and the door slightly open. Remove after 5 minutes and leave on a bench to cool.

Pipe a small amount of the hazelnut praline cream onto half the cooled meringues. Place another meringue on top to make the macaroons.

to serve
Place two scoops of the ice cream into each serving glass. Place a shot of espresso and a shot of the liqueur to the side, along with the macaroons.

When serving, pour the espresso and the liqueur over the ice cream.

note: Instead of making our Vanilla Ice Cream, you can simply use a good ready-made one.

BISCOTTI

makes 40–50 biscuits

ingredients

240 g (8½ oz) free-range egg whites
240 g (8½ oz) sugar
240 g (8½ oz) plain (all-purpose) flour
115 g (4 oz) roasted hazelnuts
115 g (4 oz) toasted pistachio nuts
50 g (1¾ oz/⅓ cup) chopped dark
    chocolate

method

Preheat the oven to 170°C (325°F/Gas 3). Line a regular-sized baking tray with baking paper.

Place the egg whites in the bowl of an electric mixer and whisk until they begin to form very soft peaks. Slowly add the sugar while whisking.

When the mixture reaches a soft peak, mix in the flour, nuts and chocolate on medium speed until combined.

Evenly fill the prepared trays with the mixture and bake for 25–35 minutes, or until the top is golden. Check that the mixture is cooked by inserting a paring knife, which should come out clean.

Remove from the oven and allow to cool on the trays for a few minutes, before turning onto a wire rack to cool completely.

Transfer to airtight containers and store in the refrigerator. The biscotti will keep for up to 3 days.

to serve

Thinly slice the biscotti using a meat slicer or a sharp knife and dry in the oven at 130°C (250°F/Gas 1) for 15–20 minutes.

Carefully transfer to serving plates — the biscotti will be very fragile.

AMARETTI BISCUITS

method

Preheat the oven to 170°C (325°F/Gas 3). Line a baking tray with baking paper.

Whisk the eggs and sugar in a bowl until pale in colour.

Sift the almond meal, flour and baking powder together, then fold into the egg mixture.

Add the melted butter and liqueur and fold in gently.

Using a teaspoon, place small heaps of the mixture on the baking tray, about 2 cm (¾ inch) apart, as they will expand during cooking.

Bake for 15 minutes, or until golden brown. Remove from the oven and cool on a wire rack.

The biscuits will keep for 2–3 days in an airtight container.

ingredients

2 free-range eggs
250 g (9 oz) caster (superfine) sugar
125 g (4½ oz/1¼ cups) almond meal
225 g (8 oz/1½ cups) plain (all-purpose) flour
1 teaspoon baking powder
25 g (1 oz) unsalted butter, melted
50 ml (1¾ fl oz) Amaretto or other almond-flavoured liqueur

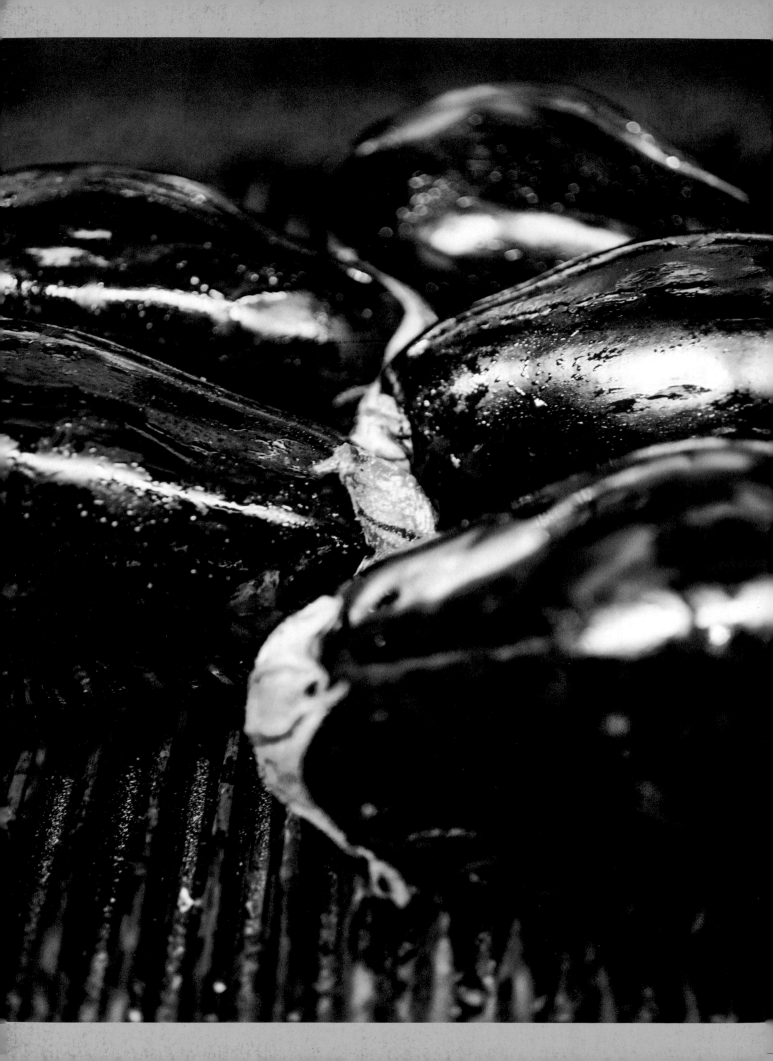

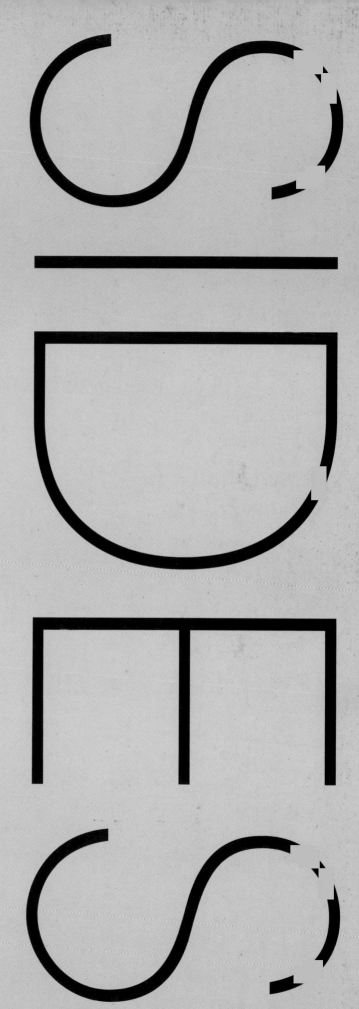

SIDES

I think it's important for any cook to have a good selection of side recipes in their repertoire, making it easy to add a variety of different flavours and textures to a whole range of meat and seafood dishes.

The side recipes gathered together in this chapter work perfectly with many of the main dishes in this book, and are ideal when meals are being shared among friends.

BRUSSELS SPROUTS WITH BACON & ROSEMARY

serves 4

method

Preheat the oven to 180°C (350°F/Gas 4).

Remove the outer layer from the brussels sprouts and discard. Cut the sprouts in half. Wash the sprouts, then leave in a colander to drain off the excess water.

Heat a large ovenproof frying pan over medium–high heat. Add the butter and olive oil. Add the sprouts and cook for 3–4 minutes, then add the bacon, shallot and rosemary and cook for a further 3 minutes.

Transfer the pan to the oven. Bake for 6–8 minutes, or until the sprouts are tender and nicely coloured.

Sprinkle with the lemon juice and season with sea salt and freshly ground black pepper. Place in a warm serving dish and serve.

ingredients

600g (1 lb 5 oz) brussels sprouts
30 g (1 oz) unsalted butter
1 tablespoon extra virgin olive oil
2 bacon rashers, rind removed, sliced
8 French shallots, thinly sliced
6 rosemary sprigs, picked
juice of ½ lemon

BAKED CELERIAC

serves 4

method

Preheat the oven to 170°C (325°F/Gas 3).

Thoroughly wash each celeriac and pat dry. Leaving them whole, brush the outsides with the olive oil, sprinkle liberally with sea salt and individually wrap each one in foil.

Place on a baking tray and bake for 2½–3 hours, depending on the size of the celeriac, until the inside is tender.

Cut them in half, scoop out the flesh and place in a warm serving bowl. Add the butter and lemon juice and mash with a fork until you have a nice crushed look.

Season with sea salt and freshly ground black pepper and serve.

ingredients

2 celeriac
60 ml (2 fl oz/¼ cup) extra virgin olive oil
50 g (1¾ oz) butter
juice of ½ lemon

ROASTED HEIRLOOM CARROTS WITH DUKKAH

serves 4

ingredients
8 baby yellow heirloom carrots
8 baby purple heirloom carrots
8 baby orange heirloom carrots
50 ml (1¾ fl oz) extra virgin olive oil
100 g (3½ oz) unsalted butter
3 tablespoons dukkah (see note)

method
Preheat the oven to 170°C (325°F/Gas 3).

Wash the carrots, lightly trimming the tops. Pat dry with a clean cloth.

Heat a large ovenproof frying pan over medium heat. Add the olive oil and carrots and cook for 3 minutes, or until coloured. Turn the carrots and season with sea salt and freshly ground black pepper.

Transfer the pan to the oven. Bake the carrots for 5 minutes, then add the butter and bake for a further 3 minutes, or until the carrots are cooked all the way through and golden in colour.

Sprinkle the carrots with the dukkah. Place in a warm serving dish and serve.

note: Dukkah is an Egyptian blend of coarsely ground toasted nuts and spices such as cumin and coriander. You'll find it in spice shops and good food stores.

SWEDE MASH

serves 4

ingredients
600 g (1 lb 5 oz) swedes (rutabaga), peeled and chopped into large chunks
1 teaspoon sea salt
40 g (1½ oz) unsalted butter
100 ml (3½ fl oz) thick (double) cream

method
Place the swede in a saucepan and cover with cold water. Add the salt and bring to a simmer. Cook for 10–15 minutes, or until tender.

Drain the swede, place in a food processor with the butter and cream and whiz to a smooth consistency.

Generously season with sea salt and freshly ground black pepper. Transfer to a warm serving bowl and serve.

ROASTED POTATO MASH

serves 4

method

Preheat the oven to 180°C (350°F/Gas 4).

Combine the potatoes and rock salt on a baking tray. Roast for 1–1½ hours, depending on their size, until a sharp knife pierces straight through.

Remove the potatoes from the oven. Cut them in half, then scoop out the flesh. Place the flesh in a mouli or potato ricer and squeeze it out into a clean saucepan.

Place the pan over medium heat. Add the milk, cream and butter and work them through the mash using a rubber spatula. Season with sea salt and freshly ground black pepper.

Scoop the mash into a warm serving bowl, drizzle with olive oil and serve.

note: You will need a hand-held mouli for this recipe.

ingredients

6 large desiree potatoes
300 g (10½ oz) rock salt
80 ml (2½ fl oz/⅓ cup) milk
100 ml (3½ fl oz) thin (pouring) cream
100 g (3½ oz) unsalted butter
extra virgin olive oil, for drizzling

GREEN BEANS WITH CONFIT SHALLOTS & TOASTED ALMONDS

serves 4

method

Heat the olive oil in a large saucepan over low heat. Add the shallot and cook for 15 minutes, or until tender.

Meanwhile, add the beans to a saucepan of salted simmering water. Cover and cook for 5–6 minutes, or until just tender, ensuring not to overcook them.

Drain the beans in a colander, then place in a mixing bowl.

Add the shallot and oil mixture to the beans, then add the toasted almonds and mix through.

Season with sea salt and freshly ground black pepper. Transfer to a warm serving bowl and serve.

ingredients

60 ml (2 fl oz/¼ cup) extra virgin olive oil
4 French shallots, finely diced
600 g (1 lb 5 oz) baby green beans, ends trimmed
35 g (1¼ oz/¼ cup) toasted slivered almonds

MUSHY PEAS WITH MINT SAUCE

serves 4

ingredients
400 g (14 oz/2¾ cups) frozen peas
100 g (3½ oz) butter
4 tablespoons mint, chopped

mint sauce
50 g (1¾ oz/¼ cup) demerara sugar
150 ml (5 fl oz) malt vinegar
1 cup roughly chopped mint leaves,
    with stalks

for the mint sauce
Place the sugar and vinegar in a saucepan and bring to the boil. Remove from the heat, add the mint leaves and stalks and cover with plastic wrap.

When the vinegar has cooled to room temperature, remove the plastic wrap and strain the mixture through a sieve, into a clean container.

Serve at room temperature.

for the mushy peas
Thaw the peas by running them under cold water. Drain the peas, then place in a blender and pulse to roughly chop the peas, without puréeing them.

Place the peas in a saucepan and cook over medium heat for 5–7 minutes, or until the peas are hot.

Add the butter and mix until it has emulsified with the peas. Stir in the chopped mint. Season with sea salt and freshly ground black pepper.

to serve
Transfer the peas to a warm serving dish. Pour the mint sauce over and serve.

ROCKET, PEAR & BLUE CHEESE SALAD WITH WALNUTS

serves 4

method

In a large mixing bowl, lightly toss the rocket, pear and walnuts together. Crumble the blue cheese into the bowl.

Add enough of the verjuice dressing to lightly coat the salad, ensuring not to overdress.

Transfer to a serving bowl and serve.

ingredients

150 g (5½ oz) wild rocket
    (arugula) leaves
1 ripe pear, sliced
24 toasted walnuts
80 g (2¾ oz) good-quality blue cheese
100 ml (3½ fl oz) Verjuice Dressing
    (see recipe on page 202)

SAUTÉED SPINACH

serves 4

method

Rinse the spinach thoroughly in cold water to ensure it is completely clean.

Transfer to a salad spinner and spin dry, leaving just a little water clinging to the leaves.

Heat the olive oil in a very large saucepan. Add the garlic and sauté over medium heat for about 1 minute, without browning.

Add the spinach and butter and season with sea salt and freshly ground black pepper. Toss through, then cover and cook for 2 minutes.

Remove the lid and increase the heat to high. Cook the spinach for another minute, stirring with a wooden spoon, until all the spinach has wilted.

Using a slotted spoon, transfer the spinach to a warm serving bowl. Drizzle with the lemon juice, sprinkle with sea salt and serve hot.

ingredients

600 g (1 lb 5 oz) baby spinach leaves,
    or large English spinach
2 tablespoons extra virgin olive oil
2 tablespoons chopped garlic
40 g (1½ oz) unsalted butter
juice of ½ lemon

PARSNIP PURÉE

serves 4

ingredients
8 parsnips
100 g (3½ oz) butter
50 ml (1¾ fl oz) extra virgin olive oil
200 ml (7 fl oz) milk
200 ml (7 fl oz) thin (pouring) cream

method
Peel the parsnips and cut into quarters lengthways, remove the core with a knife and cut widthways in half once.

Place a large saucepan over medium heat. Add the butter and olive oil. Add the parsnips and cook, stirring, for 2–3 minutes. Reduce the heat to low, then cover and cook for 8–10 minutes without colouring.

Stir in the milk and cream and continue cooking slowly, without the lid, for a further 5–7 minutes, until the parsnip has softened right down.

Transfer the mixture to a blender and blend until very smooth. Season with sea salt and freshly ground black pepper.

Transfer to a warm serving bowl and serve.

CAULIFLOWER PURÉE

serves 4

ingredients
100 g (3½ oz) butter
50 ml (1¾ fl oz) extra virgin olive oil
½ cauliflower, chopped
200 ml (7 fl oz) thin (pouring) cream

method
Place a large saucepan over medium heat. Add the butter and olive oil. Add the cauliflower and sweat for 8–10 minutes, or until tender, without colouring, with the lid on, stirring at 1 minute intervals.

Add the cream, then cover and cook over low heat for a further 8–10 minutes, or until the cauliflower is very tender.

Transfer the mixture to a blender and blend until very smooth. Season with sea salt and freshly ground black pepper.

Transfer to a warm serving bowl and serve.

GREEK SALAD

for the roasted red onion
Preheat the oven to 170°C (325°F/Gas 3).

Cut the onion in half lengthways, leaving the skin on. Place the onion halves on a baking tray, flat side down. Drizzle with the olive oil and vinegar and season with sea salt and freshly ground black pepper. Cover with foil and roast for 30–45 minutes, or until tender.

Remove from the oven and leave to cool. Remove the skin, then cut the onion halves in half again. Break up the petals and place in a mixing bowl.

for the salad
Add the tomatoes to the roasted onion, along with the cucumber, oregano, peppers, olives and feta. Season with sea salt and freshly ground black pepper.

for the dressing
Whisk together the vinegar and olive oil.

to serve
Drizzle the dressing over the salad. Transfer to a platter or bowl and serve.

ingredients
1 Roasted Red Onion
(see recipe below)
6 heirloom tomatoes, diced
1 telegraph (long) cucumber, peeled and diced
2 tablespoons oregano leaves
150 g (5½ oz) tin piquillo peppers, drained and quartered
80 g (2¾ oz) pitted kalamata olives
250 g (9 oz) Greek feta cheese

roasted red onion
1 large red onion
1½ tablespoons extra virgin olive oil
80 ml (2½ fl oz/⅓ cup) balsamic vinegar

dressing
1½ tablespoons cabernet sauvignon vinegar or red wine vinegar
100 ml (3½ fl oz) extra virgin olive oil

ZUCCHINI WITH BACON, PARMESAN & LEMON THYME

serves 4

ingredients
1 tablespoon extra virgin olive oil
4 green zucchini (courgettes), cut into
    large batons
2 rindless bacon rashers, thinly sliced
20 g (¾ oz) unsalted butter
2 lemon thyme sprigs
50 g (1¾ oz/½ cup) finely grated
    parmesan cheese

method
Heat a frying pan over medium–high heat. Add the olive oil and zucchini and cook for 4–5 minutes, or until golden in colour, adding the bacon and butter halfway through.

Add the thyme and season with sea salt and freshly ground black pepper. Remove the mixture from the pan and strain.

Transfer to a warm serving dish, sprinkle with the parmesan and serve.

ZUCCHINI SLICE

serves 6

ingredients
20 g (¾ oz) butter
1 onion, diced
2 rindless bacon rashers, chopped
3 large green zucchini (courgettes),
    about 400 g (14 oz) in total, grated
40 g (1½ oz/½ cup) grated pecorino
    cheese
40 g (1½ oz/½ cup) grated parmesan
    cheese
125 g (4½ oz) self-raising flour
4 free-range eggs

method
Preheat the oven to 180°C (350°F/Gas 4). Grease a shallow tin, measuring about 21 x 11 cm (8¼ x 4¼ inches) and 7 cm (2¾ inches) deep.

Melt the butter in a frying pan over low heat, add the onion and gently soften for 5 minutes, or until it becomes translucent.

Add the bacon and continue to cook for a few minutes. Remove from the heat and allow to cool, then transfer the mixture to a mixing bowl. Add the zucchini, cheeses and flour and mix together.

Crack the eggs into a bowl and beat lightly, then add to the zucchini mixture and stir through. Lightly season with sea salt and freshly ground black pepper.

Pour into the prepared tin and bake for 30 minutes. Serve hot or cold.

ROASTED CURRIED PUMPKIN WITH FETA & CORIANDER

serves 4

method

Preheat the oven to 170°C (325°F/Gas 3).

Peel the pumpkin, chop into large cubes and discard the seeds. Place the pumpkin in a bowl. Add the olive oil and curry spice, season with sea salt and freshly ground black pepper and mix through.

Arrange the pumpkin on a roasting tray and bake for 25–30 minutes, or until the pumpkin is golden in colour and just tender, turning a few times during cooking.

Transfer the pumpkin to a warm serving bowl or platter. Crumble the feta over the top and scatter with the coriander. Drizzle with the curry dressing and serve.

ingredients

600 g (1 lb 5 oz) butternut pumpkin (squash)

80 ml (2½ fl oz/⅓ cup) extra virgin olive oil

2 tablespoons Malay curry spice

100 g (3½ oz) marinated feta cheese, (see recipe on page 12), or any good-quality marinated feta

3 tablespoons chopped coriander (cilantro) leaves

½ quantity Curry Dressing (see recipe on page 201)

I think with any good cookbook you need a collection of good basic recipes — fantastic stocks, sauces and dressings are always great to have on hand.

Keep in mind that the recipes in this chapter are only a guide and you can adjust them, to a certain degree, to suit your personal taste.

When I was a kid, my mum would always make her own chicken stock for her soups. She would cook it overnight on a very low heat to allow all the flavours to develop, and by the morning this amazing smell of chicken stock was all through the house. She would strain the stock and come dinner time, we would all sit down to an incredibly good soup.

I often get home to Melbourne to see my mum, and even today her soup is always my first request.

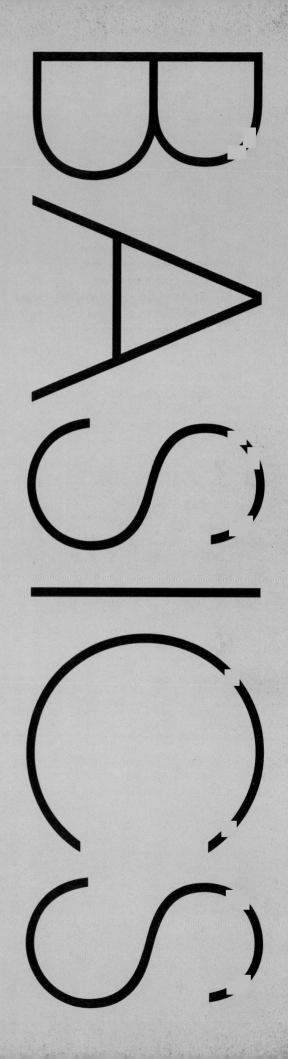

CHICKEN STOCK

makes 3–4 litres (105–140 fl oz/12–16 cups)

ingredients

4 kg (9 lb) chicken carcasses,
   rinsed and chopped
1 large onion, quartered
2 carrots, quartered
2 celery stalks, roughly chopped
1 leek, white part only, chopped
10 garlic cloves, bruised with the
   side of a knife
2 fresh bay leaves
10 thyme sprigs
5 parsley sprigs
1 teaspoon black peppercorns

method

Place all the ingredients in a large stockpot; add enough water to just cover the bones.

Heat the stock to just before boiling point, then reduce the heat to medium–low.

Simmer, uncovered, for 1½ hours, skimming the froth occasionally.

Remove from the heat and allow to stand for a few minutes, then strain through a fine sieve. Discard the solids.

Leave the stock to cool, then refrigerate or freeze in convenient portions in airtight containers.

Use fresh stock within 5 days, or freeze for up to 3 months.

BEEF STOCK

method

Preheat the oven to 180°C (350°F/Gas 4). Place a large roasting tin in the oven to heat for 5 minutes.

Add the beef bones to the roasting tin and roast, stirring frequently, for 40–50 minutes, or until golden brown.

Meanwhile, warm the olive oil in a medium stockpot over medium heat. Add the celery, leek, onion, mushrooms and carrot and cook for about 6 minutes. Stir in the tomato paste, tomatoes, parsley, peppercorns, garlic, thyme, bay leaves and wine and bring to the boil. Reduce the heat to a simmer, then cook for a further 15 minutes.

Add the beef bones, and enough water to cover the bones by 2.5 cm (1 inch). Bring to the boil, then reduce the heat to a simmer. Cook for 4–5 hours, skimming the froth occasionally.

Remove from the heat and allow to stand for a few minutes, before passing through a fine sieve. Discard the solids.

Leave the stock to cool, then refrigerate or freeze in convenient portions in airtight containers.

Use fresh stock within 5 days, or freeze for up to 3 months.

ingredients

3 kg (6 lb 12 oz) beef bones,
   cut into 6 cm (2½ inch) pieces
200 ml (7 fl oz) olive oil
3 celery stalks, chopped
2 leeks, white part only, chopped
2 onions, chopped
200 g (7 oz) button mushrooms,
   chopped
2 carrots, chopped
300 g (10½ oz) tomato paste
   (concentrated purée)
5 tomatoes, chopped
5 parsley sprigs
1 teaspoon black peppercorns
2 garlic bulbs, chopped in half
   crossways
10 thyme sprigs
3 fresh bay leaves
750 ml (26 fl oz/3 cups) red wine

LAMB STOCK

makes 3–4 litres (105–140 fl oz/12–16 cups)

ingredients

3 kg (6 lb 12 oz) lamb rib or neck bones
100 ml (3½ fl oz) olive oil
3 onions, roughly chopped
4 carrots, roughly chopped
3 celery stalks, roughly chopped
5 whole tomatoes
6 garlic cloves
3 tablespoons tomato paste
   (concentrated purée)
300 ml (10½ fl oz) dry white wine
2 teaspoons black peppercorns
4 fresh bay leaves
10 thyme sprigs
5 flat-leaf (Italian) parsley sprigs

method

Preheat the oven to 180°C (350°F/Gas 4). Place a large roasting tin in the oven to heat for 5 minutes.

Add the lamb bones to the roasting tin and roast, stirring frequently, for 40–50 minutes, or until golden brown.

Meanwhile, heat the olive oil in a large stockpot over medium–high heat. Add the vegetables and garlic and cook, stirring occasionally, for 8–10 minutes, or until the vegetables are golden brown. Stir in the tomato paste and cook for 3 minutes.

Pour in the wine and boil until the liquid has reduced by two-thirds.

Add the lamb bones, and enough water to cover the bones by 2.5 cm (1 inch). Return to the boil, then reduce the heat to a simmer, skimming off the froth that rises to the surface.

Add the peppercorns and herbs and cook for 4–6 hours, skimming the froth occasionally.

Remove from the heat and allow to stand for a few minutes, before passing through a fine sieve. Discard the solids.

Leave the stock to cool, then refrigerate or freeze in convenient portions in airtight containers.

Use fresh stock within 5 days, or freeze for up to 3 months.

VEAL STOCK

makes 3–3.5 litres (105–122 fl oz/12–14 cups)

method

Preheat the oven to 180°C (350°F/Gas 4). Place a large roasting tin in the oven to heat for 5 minutes.

Add the veal bones to the roasting tin and roast, stirring frequently, for 40–50 minutes, or until golden brown.

Meanwhile, warm the olive oil in a medium stockpot over medium heat. Add the celery, onion and carrot and cook for about 6 minutes. Stir in the tomato paste, peppercorns, garlic, thyme, bay leaves and wine and bring to the boil. Reduce the heat to a simmer, then cook for a further 15 minutes.

Add the veal bones, and enough water to cover the bones by 2.5 cm (1 inch). Return to the boil, then reduce the heat to a simmer. Cook for 3–4 hours, skimming the froth occasionally.

Remove from the heat and allow to stand for a few minutes, before passing through a fine sieve. Discard the solids.

Leave the stock to cool, then refrigerate or freeze in convenient portions in airtight containers.

Use fresh stock within 5 days, or freeze for up to 3 months.

ingredients

2 kg (4 lb 8 oz) veal bones
80 ml (2½ fl oz/⅓ cup) olive oil
4 celery stalks, roughly chopped
2 onions, skin on, cut into quarters
5 carrots, roughly chopped
400 g (14 oz) tomato paste
   (concentrated purée)
2 tablespoons black peppercorns
10 garlic cloves, smashed
10 thyme sprigs
4 fresh bay leaves
750 ml (26 fl oz/3 cups) red wine

FISH STOCK

makes 3 litres (105 fl oz/12 cups)

ingredients

2 kg (4 lb 8 oz) snapper heads,
    washed well
1 large onion, thinly sliced
2 leeks, white part only, thinly sliced
2 celery stalks, thinly sliced
½ fennel bulb, finely chopped
a splash of extra virgin olive oil
300 ml (10½ fl oz) dry white wine
5 flat-leaf (Italian) parsley sprigs
6 thyme sprigs
2 fresh bay leaves

method

To clean the snapper heads, cut around the pointed underside of the head and the gills, then pull away the bottom section of the head and discard. Scrape out any trace of blood or innards, then rinse the heads carefully.

Place all the vegetables in a stockpot. Add the olive oil and sweat the vegetables over low heat for 2 minutes without browning.

Add the fish heads and sweat them for a further minute, then increase the heat to high, pour in the wine and boil vigorously for a few minutes.

Pour in 3 litres (105 fl oz/12 cups) cold water, then add the herbs and simmer gently over low heat for 20 minutes, without allowing the stock to boil at any stage — the stock will become cloudy if boiled.

Strain the contents through a fine sieve or a colander lined with muslin (cheesecloth) to ensure the stock is clear. Discard the solids.

Leave the stock to cool, then refrigerate or freeze in convenient portions in airtight containers.

Use fresh stock within 3 days, or freeze for up to 3 months.

note: A good fish stock will set into a jelly after refrigeration.

PORK STOCK

method

Preheat the oven to 180°C (350°F/Gas 4). Place a large roasting tin in the oven to heat for 5 minutes.

Add the pork bones and ribs to the roasting tin and roast, stirring frequently, for 30–40 minutes, or until golden brown.

Meanwhile, warm the olive oil in a medium stockpot over medium heat. Add the celery, carrots, onion and garlic and cook for about 6 minutes.

Add the peppercorns, thyme, bay leaves and white and red wine and bring to the boil. Reduce the heat and simmer for about 15 minutes.

Add the roasted bones and the pig's trotters. Pour in enough water to cover the bones by 2.5 cm (1 inch) and bring to the boil. Reduce the heat to a simmer and cook for 4–5 hours, skimming the froth occasionally.

Remove from the heat and allow to stand for a few minutes, before passing through a fine sieve. Discard the solids.

Leave the stock to cool, then refrigerate or freeze in convenient portions in airtight containers.

Use fresh stock within 3 days, or freeze for up to 3 months.

ingredients

2 kg (4 lb 8 oz) pork bones

1 kg (2 lb 4 oz) pork spare ribs, cut into individual bones

60 ml (2 fl oz/¼ cup) olive oil

2 celery stalks

2 carrots, peeled

2 onions, quartered

6 garlic cloves, crushed

1 tablespoon black peppercorns

5 thyme sprigs

6 fresh bay leaves

300 ml (10½ fl oz) white wine

500 ml (17 fl oz/2 cups) red wine

2 pig's trotters, split in half (ask your butcher to do this for you)

LAMB SAUCE

makes 1 litre (35 fl oz/4 cups)

ingredients

100 ml (3½ fl oz) olive oil
500 g (1 lb 2 oz) lamb bones, chopped into small pieces
6 French shallots, skin on, roughly chopped
1 celery stalk, roughly chopped
1 carrot, roughly chopped
6 garlic cloves, crushed with the back of a knife
3 roma (plum) tomatoes, roughly chopped
1 teaspoon black peppercorns
300 ml (10½ fl oz) dry white wine
300 ml (10½ fl oz) red wine
10 thyme sprigs
3 rosemary sprigs
1 litre (35 fl oz/4 cups) Lamb Stock (see recipe on page 194)

method

Heat a stockpot over high heat, adding the olive oil and the lamb bones. Cook for 8–10 minutes, or until the lamb bones are golden brown.

Add the shallot, celery, carrot and garlic and cook for a further 5–8 minutes, or until lightly browned.

Add the tomatoes and peppercorns and cook for a further 5 minutes, stirring continuously, until most of the moisture has evaporated.

Add the white and red wine, thyme and rosemary and cook until the mixture turns syrupy.

Pour in the stock and bring to the boil. Reduce the heat and gently simmer for 20 minutes, or until the liquid has reduced by half, skimming off any fat that rises to the surface.

Remove from the heat and allow to stand for a few minutes. Pass the liquid through a fine sieve, into a suitably sized saucepan. Discard the solids.

Skim off any fat, then reheat the lamb sauce over medium heat. Use as required.

Refrigerate the fresh sauce in an airtight container for up to 5 days, or freeze for up to 3 months.

MADEIRA SAUCE

makes 1 litre (35 fl oz/4 cups)

method

Add the olive oil to a very hot saucepan. Add the meat trimmings and cook over high heat for 8–10 minutes, or until browned, turning often.

Add the shallot and the garlic and cook, stirring, for 3–4 minutes. Add the carrot, leek, celery, bay leaves, thyme and peppercorns and cook for a further 5 minutes.

Before adding the cognac, tip the saucepan a little to one side, keeping the saucepan at a safe distance from you.

With a firelighter, light the inside of the saucepan, about 2.5 cm (1 inch) from the alcohol. Quickly remove your hand and lighter from the saucepan and place the saucepan back on the stove. Cook until the flames have died out; this will mean that the alcohol has burned off.

Add the madeira and wine and cook until the mixture becomes syrupy and has reduced down by about three-quarters.

Now add the stock. Transfer to a deep saucepan, simmer and reduce down by at least half, skimming off any fat or impurities from the surface; this will take about 15 minutes.

Strain through a fine sieve, then through a colander lined with muslin (cheesecloth), into a clean saucepan.

Bring back to the boil, then reduce for a few more minutes, or until the sauce is slightly thickened and coats the back of a spoon.

Season with sea salt if needed and serve as required.

The sauce will keep in an airtight container in the fridge for 5–7 days, or can be frozen for up to 3 months.

ingredients

100 ml (3½ fl oz) olive oil
500 g (1 lb 2 oz) beef trimmings, roughly chopped
200 g (7 oz) French shallots, skins on, halved
1 garlic bulb, cut in half crossways
¼ carrot, diced
¼ leek, white part only, diced
½ celery stalk, diced
2 fresh bay leaves
5 thyme sprigs
½ teaspoon black peppercorns
100 ml (3½ fl oz) cognac
300 ml (10½ fl oz) madeira
500 ml (17 fl oz/2 cups) red wine
1 litre (35 fl oz/4 cups) Veal Stock (see recipe on page 195)

BÉARNAISE SAUCE

makes 300 ml (10½ fl oz)

tarragon reduction
2 tablespoons extra virgin olive oil
3 French shallots, chopped
2 garlic cloves, sliced
300 ml (10½ fl oz) white wine
500 ml (17 fl oz/2 cups) tarragon
    vinegar
1 heaped tablespoon dried tarragon
    leaves
4 fresh bay leaves
1 teaspoon white peppercorns
12 fresh tarragon sprigs

béarnaise sauce
3 free-range egg yolks
1½ tablespoons Tarragon Reduction
    (see recipe above)
250 g (9 oz) clarified butter (ghee),
    warmed
a pinch of cayenne pepper
6 fresh tarragon sprigs, chopped
juice of ½ lemon

for the tarragon reduction
Place a saucepan over medium heat. Add the olive oil and lightly sauté the shallot and the garlic for 3 minutes without browning. Add the wine, vinegar, dried tarragon, bay leaves and peppercorns and cook until reduced down by at least three-quarters.

Add the fresh tarragon and turn off the heat. Transfer to a clean container, cover with plastic wrap and cool overnight in the refrigerator. Strain the liquid before using.

Any leftover reduction can be kept in an airtight container in the fridge for up to 3 months.

for the béarnaise sauce
Place the egg yolks and tarragon reduction in a clean metal bowl. Set the bowl over a saucepan of simmering water, then begin whisking at 30 second intervals, taking the bowl off and on the heat, until the sabayon holds a figure eight for more than 6 seconds.

Slowly stir in the warm clarified butter; if the mixture is too thick, add a little hot water to thin it out. Season with sea salt, freshly ground black pepper and the cayenne pepper. Stir in the tarragon, and a little lemon juice to taste.

The sauce can be kept in a warm area for up to 2 hours, but no longer.

GREEN GODDESS DRESSING

makes about 400 ml (14 fl oz)

ingredients
½ cup chopped flat-leaf (Italian) parsley
6 anchovy fillets, finely chopped
2 Garlic Confit cloves (see recipe on
    page 208), chopped
2 tablespoons chopped tarragon
125 g (4½ oz/½ cup) sour cream
125 g (4½ oz/½ cup) crème fraîche
2 tablespoons lemon juice

method
In a blender, combine the parsley, anchovies, garlic and tarragon and process to a fine paste.

Transfer to a bowl, then fold in the sour cream, crème fraîche and lemon juice. Season with sea salt and freshly ground black pepper.

The dressing can be stored in an airtight container in the fridge for 2–3 days.

HONEY THYME DRESSING

makes about 250 ml (9 fl oz/1 cup)

method

Place the honey, chardonnay, thyme sprigs and 200 ml (7 fl oz) water in a saucepan over medium heat. Stir, then cook until reduced down by one-third. Remove from the heat and allow to cool slightly.

Pass the warm mixture through a sieve, into a bowl.

Slowly whisk in the olive oil, ensuring the honey is still warm so that it will emulsify. Stir in the thyme leaves and use as required.

The dressing can be kept in the fridge for up to 2 weeks in an airtight container. Serve the dressing at room temperature.

ingredients

100 ml (3½ fl oz) honey
100 ml (3½ fl oz) chardonnay
10 thyme sprigs
150 ml (5 fl oz) extra virgin olive oil
1 tablespoon thyme leaves

CURRY DRESSING

makes about 250 ml (9 fl oz/1 cup)

for the curry oil

In a frying pan, lightly toast the curry powder over medium heat for 2 minutes, or until fragrant.

Add the olive oil. Turn down the heat, then slowly bring back to a warm heat.

Remove from the heat, allow to cool, then pour into a clean airtight container and leave for 24 hours.

Pass through filter paper before using.

for the curry dressing

Mix the curry oil and vinegar together in a clean, sealed jar, shaking well. Use as required.

The dressing can be refrigerated in an airtight container for up to 3 months.

curry oil

2 teaspoons curry powder
200 ml (7 fl oz) olive oil

curry dressing

200 ml (7 fl oz) Curry Oil (see recipe above)
50 ml (1¾ fl oz) cabernet sauvignon vinegar or red wine vinegar

VERJUICE DRESSING

makes 1 litre (35 fl oz/4 cups)

ingredients
4 tablespoons dijon mustard
1 tablespoon balsamic vinegar
500 ml (17 fl oz/2 cups) verjuice
400 ml (14 fl oz) olive oil

method
In a bowl, combine the mustard, vinegar and verjuice.

Begin mixing with a hand-held blender while slowly adding the olive oil.

Season with sea salt and freshly ground black pepper and use as required.

The dressing can be kept in the fridge for up to 2 weeks in an airtight container. Serve the dressing at room temperature.

note: Verjuice (`green juice' in French) is the juice of unripe grapes or other fruit. It is sold in bottles in fine food stores.

TRUFFLE VERJUICE DRESSING

makes about 1 litre (35 fl oz/4 cups)

ingredients
4 tablespoons dijon mustard
1 tablespoon balsamic vinegar
500 ml (17 fl oz/2 cups) verjuice
400 ml (14 fl oz) olive oil
100 ml (3½ fl oz) truffle oil

method
In a bowl, combine the mustard, vinegar and verjuice.

Begin mixing with a hand-held blender while slowly adding the olive oil.

Slowly add the truffle oil, then season with sea salt and freshly ground black pepper and use as required.

The dressing can be kept in the fridge for up to 2 weeks in an airtight container. Serve the dressing at room temperature.

LIME PICKLE

method

Cut each lime into eight wedges, place in a bowl and sprinkle with the salt. Cover and set aside in a cool dry place for 2 days, stirring occasionally.

Heat the oil in a medium saucepan over medium heat. Add the mustard seeds and cook for 30 seconds, or until the seeds begin to pop.

Add the garlic, ginger, cumin, coriander and chilli powder and cook, stirring, for 30 seconds, or until aromatic.

Stir in 200 ml (7 fl oz) water, the lime mixture, sugar and vinegar. Bring to the boil, then reduce the heat to low. Simmer, stirring occasionally, for 15 minutes, or until the mixture is thick.

Transfer to clean jars or an airtight container and set aside for 1 week to allow the flavours to develop. The pickle can be refrigerated for up to 6 months.

ingredients

10 limes
1 tablespoon sea salt
50 ml (1¾ fl oz) vegetable oil
2 tablespoons mustard seeds
4 garlic cloves, finely chopped
20 g (¾ oz) fresh ginger, peeled
    and finely chopped
1½ teaspoons ground cumin
1½ teaspoons ground coriander
½ teaspoon chilli powder
185 g (6½ oz/1 cup) soft brown sugar
1 tablespoon white vinegar

MISO BROTH

makes about 1.2 litres (42 fl oz)

method

Bring 1 litre (35 fl oz/4 cups) water to the boil in a saucepan. Slowly add the dashi and allow to dissolve.

Whisk in the miso and remove from the heat — do not allow the miso to boil.

Stir in the mustard and vinegar and use as required.

The dressing can be kept in an airtight container in the fridge for 3–5 days.

note: Dashi granules are a dried Japanese soup stock made from shaved bonito tuna and seaweed. You'll find dashi in health food stores and Asian grocers.

ingredients

1½ tablespoons dashi granules
    (see note)
1½ tablespoons white miso paste
3 teaspoons dijon mustard
1 tablespoon sherry vinegar

SUGAR SYRUP

makes 500 ml (17 fl oz/2 cups)

ingredients
250 g (9 oz) caster (superfine) sugar
250 ml (9 fl oz/1 cup) water

method
In a saucepan, bring the sugar and water to the boil. Remove from the heat and leave to cool.

Store in an airtight container in the refrigerator and use as required. The syrup will keep for up to 1 month.

SUGAR SYRUP FOR SORBETS

makes 625 ml (21½ fl oz/2½ cups)

ingredients
250 g (9 oz) caster (superfine) sugar
250 ml (9 fl oz/1 cup) water
125 g (4½ oz) glucose syrup

method
Place all the ingredients in a saucepan and bring to the boil. Remove from the heat and leave to cool.

Store in an airtight container in the refrigerator and use as required. The syrup will keep for up to 1 month.

SWEET PASTRY

method

Sift the flour and icing sugar into a large bowl.

Gradually add the butter, rubbing it in with your fingertips, until the mixture resembles breadcrumbs. (You can also use a food processor, pulsing until the mixture resembles breadcrumbs, then turn the mixture into a bowl.) Make a well in the centre and add the vanilla seeds.

Beat the egg and egg yolk together, then pour the mixture into the well.

Stir with a wooden spoon, then use your hands to mix well until the dough comes together into one ball, adding a little cold water if the dough is too dry.

Wrap in plastic wrap and allow to rest in the fridge for 30 minutes before rolling out and using as your recipe directs.

ingredients

250 g (9 oz/1⅔ cups) plain (all-purpose) flour

90 g (3¼ oz/¾ cup) icing (confectioners') sugar

125 g (4½ oz) cold unsalted butter, diced

1 vanilla bean, cut in half lengthways, seeds scraped

1 free-range egg, plus 1 free-range egg yolk

SHORTCRUST PASTRY

method

Sift the flour and salt into a large bowl.

Gradually add the butter, rubbing it in with your fingertips, until the mixture resembles breadcrumbs. (You can also use a food processor, pulsing until the mixture resembles breadcrumbs, then turn the mixture into a bowl.)

Make a well in the centre of the mixture.

Beat the eggs, then pour into the well. Add the cold water and stir a little with a wooden spoon until well combined.

Use your hands to gently bring the mixture together into one ball, adding a little extra flour if the mixture becomes sticky.

Wrap in plastic wrap and allow to rest in the fridge for 30 minutes before rolling out and using as your recipe directs.

ingredients

350 g (12 oz/2⅓ cups) plain (all-purpose) flour

a pinch of sea salt

150 g (5½ oz) cold unsalted butter, diced

2 free-range eggs

50 ml (1¾ fl oz) cold water

TART SHELLS

makes 1 large tart, or up to 25 smaller tart shells

ingredients
1 quantity of Sweet Pastry or
   Shortcrust Pastry (see recipes on
   page 205)

method
Preheat the oven to 160°C (315°F/Gas 2–3).

Roll out the rested pastry on a chilled, floured surface, to 2 mm ($\frac{1}{16}$ inch) thick. Leave as one large piece, or cut into smaller tart shapes as your recipe directs.

Ease the pastry into your desired mould or tart (flan) tin, trim the edges with a sharp knife and prick the base several times with a fork. Place in the refrigerator to rest for 30 minutes, to minimise shrinkage during blind baking.

Line the pastry with baking paper and cover with rice or dried beans. Transfer to the oven and blind bake for 5–10 minutes, depending on the size of the tart shells.

Remove the baking paper and rice or beans. Bake for a further 5–10 minutes, or until the pastry base is cooked. (Ensure the pastry base is well cooked, so that if you are adding a hot filling, the tart doesn't collapse.)

Use as your recipe directs.

note: The uncooked pastry can be kept in the freezer and transferred to the fridge overnight before using; alternatively, thaw the pastry on the bench for 1 hour before using.

CRISP SHALLOTS

makes 500 g (1 lb 2 oz)

ingredients
500 ml (17 fl oz/2 cups) vegetable oil
500 g (1 lb 2 oz) red Asian shallots or
   French shallots, thinly sliced

method
Heat the oil in a wok or saucepan over medium heat. Add half the shallot and slowly cook for 6–8 minutes, or until golden brown, stirring occasionally.

Remove with a slotted spoon, drain on paper towels and allow to cool.

Repeat with the remaining shallot.

Once cold, transfer to an airtight container. Store in a cool place for up to 4 weeks.

PASTA DOUGH

makes 500 g (1 lb 2 oz)

method

Heap the flour on the bench, in a mound.

Make a well in the middle of the flour, then add the eggs, salt, water and olive oil.

Using a fork, beat the eggs to begin incorporating them into the flour, starting with the inner rim of the well.

As the well expands, keep pushing the flour up from the base of the mound to retain the well shape. The dough will come together when half the flour is incorporated.

At this point, start kneading the dough with both hands, using the palms of your hands. Once you have a cohesive mass, remove the dough from the bench and discard any leftover bits.

Lightly re-flour the bench, then continue kneading for a further 6 minutes. The dough should be elastic and a little sticky.

Wrap the dough in plastic wrap and allow to rest for 30 minutes at room temperature.

The dough can be made up to 2 hours ahead.

ingredients

320 g (11¼ oz) '00' flour or strong flour
3 free-range eggs
a pinch of sea salt
1 teaspoon water
1 teaspoon extra virgin olive oil

MISO MAYO

makes 600 g (1 lb 5 oz)

method

Place the mustard, egg yolks, vinegar and yuzu juice in a bowl. Begin whisking while slowly adding the oil.

Whisk in the wasabi and miso until well combined.

The mayo can be stored in an airtight container in the fridge for up to 2 weeks.

notes: Yuzu is an aromatic Japanese citrus fruit. Fresh is best but can be hard to obtain; bottled yuzu juice is sold in some Japanese specialty grocers and fine food stores.

Instead of making your own mayonnaise in this recipe, you can simply mix the yuzu or lime juice, wasabi and miso paste through 400 g (14 oz) good-quality mayonnaise.

ingredients

1 tablespoon dijon mustard
2 large free-range egg yolks
2 tablespoons white wine vinegar
45 ml (1½ fl oz) yuzu juice (see notes)
    or lime juice, to taste
300 ml (10½ fl oz) vegetable oil
2 tablespoons grated fresh wasabi
    (if fresh wasabi is unavailable, use
    good-quality frozen wasabi)
70 g (2½ oz) white miso paste

ONION CONFIT

makes about 1 cup

ingredients
100 g (3½ oz) butter
2 large onions, thinly sliced
100 ml (3½ fl oz) honey
100 ml (3½ fl oz) white wine
50 ml (1¾ fl oz) sherry vinegar or
  balsamic vinegar

method
Melt the butter in a heavy-based saucepan. Add the onion and cook over low heat for 10 minutes, stirring occasionally.

Stir in the honey and wine and cook over very low heat for 45–50 minutes, or until the mixture has a jam-like consistency.

Add the vinegar and season to taste with sea salt and freshly ground black pepper.

Transfer to a sterilised jar and use as required. The confit will keep in the refrigerator for up to 2 weeks.

GARLIC CONFIT

makes 200 g (7 oz)

ingredients
200 g (7 oz) garlic cloves
600 ml (21 fl oz) milk
300 ml (10½ fl oz) extra virgin olive oil

method
Peel the garlic cloves and place in a saucepan. Cover with 200 ml (7 fl oz) of the milk. Bring to the boil, then strain.

Place the garlic back in the pan and cover with another 200 ml (7 fl oz) of the milk. Bring to the boil, then strain.

Repeat the process a third time, using the remaining milk.

Drain, then rinse the garlic in cold water. Place the garlic in a clean saucepan and cover with the olive oil. Cook the garlic very slowly for 30 minutes, or until tender.

Remove the garlic cloves with a slotted spoon, reserving the oil. Place the garlic in a blender. Begin blending, adding a little of the reserved garlic oil to form a paste. Season with sea salt and freshly ground black pepper.

Transfer to a sterilised jar and use as required. The confit will keep in the refrigerator for up to 10 days.

MANGO CHUTNEY

method

Peel the mangoes, cut the flesh away from the stones and roughly chop.

Heat the oil in a frying pan over medium heat. Add the chilli flakes and cook for 1 minute, ensuring the chilli doesn't burn.

Add the onion and sweat down for 5 minutes, or until soft. Add the ginger and capsicum and sauté for 1–2 minutes. Now add the mango and cook for a further minute.

In a separate bowl, combine the pineapple juice, vinegar, sugar and curry powder. Add this mixture to the pan and stir to combine.

Bring the mixture to a bare simmer and leave to reduce for 45–55 minutes, or until thickened, stirring frequently.

Season with sea salt and freshly ground black pepper. Stir in the raisins and macadamias and transfer to another container that is sitting over an ice bath.

Spoon the chutney into a sterilised jar and use as required. The chutney will keep in the refrigerator for up to 1 month.

ingredients

1 kg (2 lb 4 oz) mangoes, ripe but
   not too soft
1½ tablespoons vegetable oil
½ teaspoon chilli flakes, or more if
   you like it hot
1½ red onions, diced
3 tablespoons finely grated fresh ginger
1 red capsicum (pepper), diced
1.5 litres (52 fl oz/6 cups) pineapple
   juice
400 ml (14 fl oz) cider vinegar
125 g (4½ oz/⅔ cup) soft brown sugar
1 tablespoon curry powder
125 g (4½ oz/⅔ cup) raisins or
   sultanas (golden raisins)
125 g (4½ oz) roasted macadamia
   nuts, roughly chopped

INDEX

ACKNOWLEDGEMENTS

Firstly a huge thank you to my Group Head Chef, Joe Pavlovich, for working so hard on this cookbook, testing the recipes and creating some of these amazing dishes. Joe works tirelessly across all our restaurants, not only on land, but also at sea. Joe has been my longest-serving chef and I can't thank him enough for his loyalty and commitment.

Alasdair France, who has been with me since Bistro Lulu/Salt days and is now living in Singapore, as General Manager for Salt grill and Salt tapas & bar. Alasdair has had an enormous impact on our expansion, not only in Australia but throughout Asia. I cannot thank him enough for his dedication to our company.

Also to the best personal assistant anyone could have, Rebecca McNeilly, who also worked very closely with Joe and myself on perfecting the recipes so that they are clear and accessible for the home cook.

Daniel Whitelaw and Mandy Newson; Restaurant Managers for Salt grill Jakarta and Gold Coast, respectively, as well as Shehan Croner, Restaurant Manager for glass brasserie, and Ania Juszkiewicz, Restaurant Manager for Salt grill, Singapore. Your loyalty and support for the brand and your teams are second to none.

Marjon Olguera, Head Chef at our new Salt grill, Jakarta. MJ has been one of my longest-standing chefs and will have a huge influence on the creation of the menu. Head Chef Kathy Tindell, who heads up the kitchen team on the Gold Coast and has been a part of my team for well over eight years now; they have both been a great asset to the Luke Mangan group.

We have a great team of staff in Singapore, including our Head Chef, Tom Wells, who opened our first Salt grill restaurant on Pacific Jewel and has come over from our Salt tapas & bar in Singapore. Koji, our Head Chef at Salt Tokyo for creating so many amazing dishes over the years, your creativity is inspirational for those around you.

Our restaurants on board P&O would not have been such a huge success without the help and support of the Carnival Australia team: Ann Sherry, CEO; Sture Myrmell, VP to Hotel Operations; Lars Kristiansen, former Food & Beverage Director; Uwe Stiefel, Corporate Executive Chef.

Anthony Puharich, Director and good friend from Vic's Meats, your passion for quality means that we are always given the best produce, so thank you. Jules Crocker from Joto Fish for always delivering the freshest quality produce, which is evident in this cookbook.

To my good friend Adrian Lander, who worked on my first cookbook BLD back in 2000, and has again come through with the goods with his perfect photography.

To all my staff who work tirelessly day in and day out to give all our customers the best experience possible. My business partner in Asia, Seiki Takahashi, for enabling us to expand our partnership together to Tokyo, Singapore, Jakarta and now Bali.

Heath Molloy, my business partner, who oversees the product and warehouse division within our new head office, your dedication to the team does not go unnoticed. The Virgin Australia team at the Luke Mangan Headquarters in Waterloo, Sydney, also known as 'the engine room' and the location for our new wine bar, Mojo by Luke Mangan.

To my partners in Australia; Hilton Hotels, Virgin Australia, Volvo and P&O Cruises. Electrolux for supporting my vision for Appetite for Excellence, the only awards of their kind in Australia, and supporting the growth of young talent within this country.

To Phee Gardner, who has also been with me since Salt days and who now runs and operates this awards program, your commitment and passion for the program has made it what it is today.

Published in 2013 by Murdoch Books, an imprint of Allen & Unwin.

Murdoch Books Australia
83 Alexander Street
Crows Nest NSW 2065
Phone: +61 (0) 2 8425 0100
Fax: +61 (0) 2 9906 2218
www.murdochbooks.com.au
info@murdochbooks.com.au

Murdoch Books UK
Erico House, 6th Floor
93–99 Upper Richmond Road
Putney, London SW15 2TG
Phone: +44 (0) 20 8785 5995
Fax: +44 (0) 20 8785 5985
www.murdochbooks.co.uk
info@murdochbooks.co.uk

For Corporate Orders & Custom Publishing contact
Noel Hammond, National Business Development Manager, Murdoch Books Australia

Publisher: Sue Hines
Designer: Hugh Ford
Photographer: Adrian Lander
Stylist: Carlu Seaver
Editor: Katri Hilden
Project Editor: Claire Grady
Production Manager: Karen Small

A cataloguing-in-publication entry is available from the catalogue of the National Library of Australia at www.nla.gov.au.

A catalogue record for this book is available from the British Library.

Colour reproduction by Splitting Image, Clayton, Victoria

Printed by Hang Tai Printing Company, China

IMPORTANT: Those who might be at risk from the effects of salmonella poisoning (the elderly, pregnant women, young children and those suffering from immune deficiency diseases) should consult their doctor with any concerns about eating raw eggs.

OVEN GUIDE: You may find cooking times vary depending on the oven you are using. For fan-forced ovens, as a general rule, set the oven temperature to 20°C (35°F) lower than indicated in the recipe.

MEASURES GUIDE: We have used 20 ml (4 teaspoon) tablespoon measures. If you are using a 15 ml (3 teaspoon) tablespoon add an extra teaspoon of the ingredient for each tablespoon specified.

The stylist would like to thank Malcolm Greenwood for the ceramics shown in the photographs for Salt & Pepper Squid (page 17), Barbecued Prawns, Avocado & Mango Salsa (page 35), Rocket, Pear & Blue Cheese Salad with Walnuts (page 183) and Moroccan Snapper & Shellfish Hotpot with LimePickle (page 95).